O. Devereux Prece.

14 May 1971.

from Sheila & Douglas.

ARTHUR: ROMAN BRITAIN'S LAST CHAMPION

BY THE SAME AUTHOR

Poems

Devouring Zodiac

The Choice

Phoenix and Unicorn

Air Journey

Translations

Ovid on Love

Sappho of Lesbos

The Complete Works of Francois Villon (Everyman's Library)

Prose

The Christian Island

The Origins of the English People

BERAM SAKLATVALA

ARTHUR:
ROMAN BRITAIN'S
LAST CHAMPION

DAVID & CHARLES: NEWTON ABBOT

ISBN 0 7153 5201 6

First published 1967
Second impression 1968
Third impression 1971

COPYRIGHT NOTICE

Printed in Great Britain
by Redwood Press Limited Trowbridge Wilts
for David & Charles (Publishers) Limited
South Devon House Newton Abbot Devon

It is of this Arthur that the Britons fondly tell so many fables, even to the present day: a man worthy to be celebrated, not by idle fictions, but by authentic history. He long upheld the sinking state, and roused the broken spirit of his countrymen to war.

WILLIAM OF MALMESBURY
1095-1143

(ASA) FROM WALES RELIGUS SKOLER (BISHOP) ALFROAD)

(BATLE) EDINGTON ALFONY DEFEAT VICKINGS

(WHITE HORSE) WINCHESTER (CATHEDRAL)

CONTENTS

ANGLIA / WESSEX / EAST ANGLIA / MERCIA NORTHUMBLIN (WATAER)

ALFREAD) KING — BORN - 849 OXFOR) SHIRE

WESSEX

(KING) ALFREAD THE GREAT (899) DEATH
1 OLD. MINESTER RE-INT (WESSEX)
2 NEW. MINESTER (903) (EDWARD ELDER)
3 HYDE ABBE. / ALFRID AILSWORTH (110)
4 BRIDWR FARM. LAND (1538)

Dux Brittanniorum

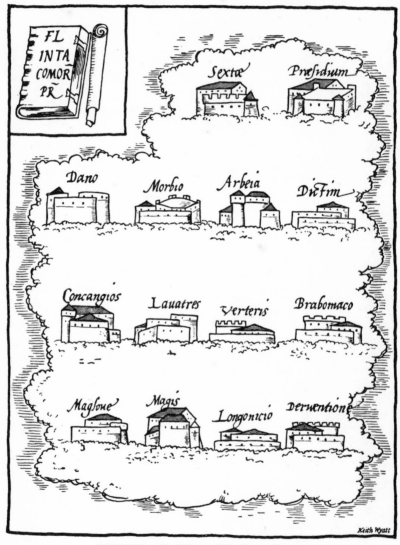

INSIGNIA OF THE DUKE OF BRITAIN
(by permission of the Bayerische Staatsbibliothek)

Descriptive Note on page 195

PREFACE

THIS book has two main themes: the fall of Roman Britain and the life of the legendary King Arthur.

The Roman power in Britain decayed by about AD 400. Some forty years later the Angles and Saxons came over from Germany and fought for possession of the country. But another hundred years or more were to pass before they firmly occupied the greater part of Britain and before the English kingdoms were truly founded.

What happened during this time? Were all the Britons—as we were once taught—slaughtered or driven into Wales? Did the inhabitants of the island, weakened by years of dependence on Rome's now-vanished power, offer no resistance to the invaders? If so, then why did the conquest of Britain by the English take so long? Moreover, in the years when Rome lay dying, what part did Britain play in Europe and what influence did she have on events in Rome itself? Finally, where are the true roots of the English people? Do they lie solely in the Anglo-Saxon folk, or does the blood of the Britons, of the Romans and of their Continental legionaries, still flow in the veins of the English and in the veins of the latters' descendants around the world? These are the questions that prompted the examination of the fall of Roman Britain.

As to the second theme, there is now general acceptance that behind the legendary figure of King Arthur there stands a real and historic personage—a great leader who was for a while the centre of the Britons' resistance, and a man who roused the broken spirits of his countrymen. He was the last champion of Roman Britain and the last successful commander of the Britons in their wars against the Anglo-Saxon invaders.

Some sixty years ago the late Professor John Rhys (in his preface to the Everyman edition of Malory's *Morte d'Arthur*) proposed that Arthur was an official of Romanised Britain, holding a formal post in its administration.

In the latter part of this book an attempt is made to investigate these matters. The earliest references to Arthur, dating from the time before the shadows of myth obscured him, are so meagre and fragmentary that no full portrait can be drawn from them. Until or unless more material comes to light, it seems that we can catch only faint glimpses of the events of his life. But though the early sources are so few, and the later sources so unreliable, I have examined them all carefully, rejecting none lightly. Even the later and more inventive writers of tale and fable claim to have drawn on earlier material. If these claims are only partly true, then each has some particle of truth to contribute. By comparing one with another, by checking the traditions of the Anglo-Saxons as recorded in their *Chronicle* with the stories told by the Britons in the pages of Gildas and Nennius, I have tried to establish a narrative that is supported by all, and conflicts with none, of the evidence. A sequence of events emerges which could have given rise both to the tales in the chronicles as well as to the main stories in the romances and legends.

The two themes are inextricably intertwined. The administrative and military organisation of Roman Britain influenced and guided the Britons long after Roman power had vanished from the island. In the story of Britain when she prospered as the Roman Island—covered in the first few chapters—can be found the precedents and examples which Arthur would have followed during his struggle against the forces of heathendom and barbarism. Because his struggle was for so long successful, we can see how the two peoples—Romanised Britons and heathen Anglo-Saxons—lived together in contact and in conflict for a century or more, each contributing to the final character of the English people.

The period covered by the narrative is the period when this

character was irrevocably formed. Later invasions of Dane and Norman were to modify this character in the ensuing centuries. But the basic reasons why the English are so different from the Germans whence they sprung, and from the Celts whom they replaced, are to be found in the events described in this book, and in the bitter struggle waged between native Briton and invading Anglo-Saxon in the days of Arthur.

B.S

I

THE ROMAN ISLAND

ARTHUR'S work was the defence of Britain, the Roman Island, against the heathen Anglo-Saxons.

For over 400 years Britain had lain under the rule of Rome. For most of that time she was a well-organised land of grey-walled cities, colonnaded buildings and neat red-tiled houses. Six thousand miles of well-planned roads ran over hill and valley. Prosperous farms were built and flourished. Tall lighthouses threw their yellow glare over the dark seas. Ships queued for berths at square jetties and neat landing wharves, bringing red pottery from France, glassware from Southern Germany, and fine wines from Italy. Silver dinner services shone on the tables of the rich, lit by hanging lamps and tall candelabra. Men worshipped Christ decently in public chapel and private room. Busy clerks sat in banks and offices, and in the government departments through which the power, wisdom and justice of Rome flowed into the land.

The lead mines of Derbyshire and the tin mines of Cornwall came under government control. The wool of the Cotswold sheep was spun and woven, and sold to the thriving towns. The primitive British plough was replaced by the more efficient wheeled implement of the Empire. Britain could feed herself, and had at one time a surplus of wheat for export to the Rhine army. Groups of ex-servicemen, settled on farms cut out of the wasteland with military and rectangular precision, gossiped in the evening of

old campaigns and of dead companions. Tax collectors made
their assessment of the crops, and collected their dues. In return
for these taxes, the people had orderly government, the protection of an efficient and well-disciplined army, good roads, a sound
currency of gold, silver and bronze, good trade, and a safe future.
The land almost lost the name of Britain, and became known as
the Roman Island.

Four hundred years is a long period, spanning twelve generations. Institutions which last so long begin to appear everlasting. Men could not remember, except through the mist of legend,
the time before the Romans came. Rome was an eternal city.
The summer of her rule seemed like the summers of our childhood—age-long and unending.

But autumn came, and the drear midwinter.

The seat of power in Rome, the title of Emperor, ceased to
be an honoured responsibility. It became a trophy to be pur-
chased or fought for by ambitious army commanders. Since
such Emperors could retain power only with the army's support,
the legions learned that it was they and not the Roman Senate
and people who were sovereign. Officers who dreamed of personal empire learned a new lesson, too : that power could be held
locally, and that a man could officially bear the title of Emperor
without ever seeing the city of Rome itself.

The barbarian people outside the Empire felt the new tide
flowing through Europe. Some had seen the changes at first
hand, having enlisted in the Roman army. They learned that
the lands of the provinces were rich, and that they could be
raided and the wealth carried away. They learned also, as they
served under the standards of Rome, something of discipline,
and much of power and of politics. Coming to serve, they learned
how to destroy.

Autumn came to the Roman Island when reckless officers in
Britain set themselves up as local Emperors. Battles were fought
again in Britain, as the central government sent expeditionary
forces to quell local usurpers. Autumn grew more chill when the

against the Germanic invaders—the Saxons and the Angles—and
that he was for a long time successful, only to die tragically in a
civil war.

To understand his work, it is necessary to look at the traditions which he inherited. We must see how the Romans came
here, how they organised the land, and what examples and precedents they set for him. These will show the means Arthur
possessed, military, spiritual and political, and set in perspective
the significance of his stand. With the clues that such a review of
the whole drama provides, some of the threads of truth that lie
entangled in the fables may be unravelled, showing something
of the historical facts about the last champion of the Roman
Island.

II

BRITAIN'S HEROES AND BRITAIN'S FAITH

AT the outset of Roman rule Britain produced two heroic figures who bravely though unsuccessfully defied their conquerors.

The first was Caractacus—whose name is an earlier form of the modern Welsh Caradoc. When, a hundred years after the unsuccessful invasion of Britain by Julius Caesar, the Emperor Claudius finally occupied the island, Caractacus fought the Romans skilfully for nine years, establishing himself in North and Central Wales. In a hard-fought battle, in which Tacitus admits there were many Roman casualties, his forces were at last destroyed and his family captured. He himself escaped but was handed over to the Roman authorities by Cartimandua, Queen of what is now Yorkshire, in whose territory he had vainly sought asylum. He was taken as a prisoner to Rome where his proud defiance of his conquerors won their respect and admiration. Tacitus recorded the story, so that it was known in Arthur's time.

Tacitus also tells us of Boudica, the widowed Queen of the Iceni, who after Claudius's death and during the reign of Nero rallied the Britons and almost swept away the Roman occupation forces. Her dead husband had made the Roman Emperor one of his heirs; the troops coming to collect the legacy flogged her, sacked her palace and raped her daughters. She mustered her followers and slaughtered the ex-servicemen settled in Camulodunum, the modern Colchester, and completely routed the Ninth Legion. The Romans retreated, allowing London to fall into her wrathful hands: the loss of a city was the price deliberately paid for the retention of the province. At London and at Verulamium (the modern St Albans), when Boudica's army entered in vengeful triumph, no prisoners were taken; the citizens were put to the sword or crucified, and the cities burned. Tacitus speaks of 70,000 dead. Below London, Colchester and St Albans the ashes still lie thick, and the spade still uncovers crumbled charcoal, fused clay, and blackened pottery—her terrible and indelible signature. Massive reinforcements came to the Roman army from the Continent, and Boudica's defeat was overwhelming. She committed suicide; but even so the British were not eager for peace.

Caradoc and Boudica must be remembered when considering the final story of Arthur, for it was their descendants who fought against the later invaders from Germany, and we should not underrate the passion and vigour of this blood: the picture usually drawn of an effete and nerveless Britain some 300 years later passively accepting slaughter and dispossession at the hands of the Saxon invaders is as incredible as it is inaccurate.

Other figures whose examples dominated men's minds, and whose stories influenced Arthur and his contemporaries included Clodius Albinus, who towards the end of the second century took the army of Britain across the Channel, declared himself Emperor and defied Rome. He was defeated and committed suicide. Britain suffered for his ambition. With its garrisons reduced, Hadrian's Wall was overrun by the northern tribes and the tide of war flowed south toward Chester and York. All was later restored; but the disastrous adventure of Albinus ought to have warned future commanders that Britain's garrisons should never be sent over into Europe.

In the third century the coasts of Britain and Gaul were being raided by pirates from Holland, Denmark and Northern Germany. The emergence into the North Sea and the Channel of these sea-borne war bands rendered the classical Roman frontier-defence system out of date. The Rhine, a natural frontier between the tough land-hungry German races and the fruitful provinces, was outflanked when the first German raider landed on the coast of Gaul or Britain, with two or three score ruffians, looted some seaside villa and slipped away before the nearest troops could arrive.

Most active and terrible of these raiders were the men of a German nation, the Saxons. They are first mentioned by Ptolemy the geographer who, writing in the second century AD, tells us that they then lived on the neck of the Cimbric peninsula, the modern Denmark. To the north lived another tribe, the Angles, first mentioned by Tacitus; these two neighbours appear to have become closely associated with one another through war or other contacts. As their raids increased, Rome realised that no body of troops, however carefully located, could guard every beach and cove of the long coastlines of northern France and of south-east Britain. The only answer would be a fleet, which could give early warning to the land forces and possibly intercept and sink the raiders before they landed.

As early as the reign of Hadrian we have evidence of the existence of units of the British fleet *(Classis Britannica)*. In the face of the new threat, this fleet was expanded, and Rome had to find a suitable naval commander. Her own military genius lay on land. She had always supplemented her own skills by using those of conquered and neighbouring people. So it was natural for her to turn to one of the maritime nations to fill this post. Carausius, from one of the seafaring tribes of the North Sea coasts, was a man of vigour and resolution, double-chinned, straggle-bearded and of low birth. His actions were to have lasting effects upon Britain's history and indeed upon the history of Rome. His headquarters were at Gessoriacum, the modern Boulogne. His task, according to Eutropius (who wrote about a century later), was to control the seas and to guard the Channel coast from the Belgian shore westwards to the Atlantic.

Carausius was successful. Eutropius tells us that he captured many of the raiding ships together with their booty. But instead of returning the plunder to the victims or to the Imperial treasury, he kept it as his own prize of war. It began to be hinted that Carausius was in league with the pirates and was sharing their loot rather than preventing their crimes. The Emperor Maximianus formally dismissed him. But with the strong weapon of the fleet under his control, and with his sea chests filled, Carausius did not submit. Instead, recognising the invincibility of Britain, provided she controlled the narrow seas, he crossed

CARAUSIUS, FROM A COIN

over from Boulogne to the island, taking the *Classis Britannica*, the British fleet, with him. For the first time in recorded history, a power in Britain, infinitely inferior to the great land powers of Europe, sat safely behind the misty Channel and defied the power of a Continental giant. And Carausius finally declared himself Emperor.

Thus Britain now had her own Imperial ruler. From London, he issued a plentiful coinage, bearing slogans and symbols of his success. On one stands the figure of Britannia, clasping Carausius by the hand. Another bears the slogan *Renovatio Romanorum*, 'The Restoration of the Romans'. Britain was having the best of both worlds: she was something of a sovereign nation-state, with her own government, and yet claimed to be a part of the greater world beyond her seas.

The Emperors in Rome, unable to break into the island fortress, recognised Carausius as a co-Emperor, and the titles he had usurped became his by right. Two vital precedents had been established: that Britain could be a self-sufficient and independent power; and that there could be a local Emperor, a Lord of Britain. This new knowledge that the Romanised area of Britain was a natural and stable political unity remained and survived into the days of England. The title of Lord of Britain *(Bretwalda)* was to be early sought by the invading English and early established. The concept of a unified and independent England owes much to the concept of a unified and independent Britain. To Carausius, buccaneer though he may have been, much is due.

To serve the fleet, ten naval bases were set up round the southern and eastern shores of Britain: Bradwell, Dover, Lympne, Brancaster, Burgh Castle, Reculver, Richborough, Pevensey, Porchester and possibly Walton Castle. Here Carausius's ships came to harbour between patrols, and here no doubt the crews took their shore leave. Here probably settled some of the first Germanic inhabitants of this island, Frank, Menapian and possibly Saxon, recruited as sailors in the British fleet. Here perhaps beer was drunk in the taverns, by throats too salt for wine; here perhaps the Germanic speech was first spoken, harsh and guttural to Roman ears; here, in a group of mercenary sailors, was the first faint shadow of England, which in five more generations was to eclipse all Roman Britain. The strip of coast where these forts stood came to be known as the Saxon Shore. The Saxon Shores, in Britain and in Gaul, were the only territories in the Empire to be named after a hostile people, and they may well have been so named because of the Saxon sailors and ex-servicemen settled there.

In AD 292 Carausius's second in command, Allectus, cast covetous eyes on the power of his commander, and the Emperors in

finally marching as a conqueror to Rome; so Britain had created her fourth Emperor, and her greatest.

A ruler from Britain had successfully invaded the Continental Empire; the armies of Britain had marched to the Eternal City itself and had made their commander the only Augustus, ruler of the world. To Britain's knowledge of security behind her moat was added a glimpse of greater possibilities—a glimpse that was to prove both dazzling and fatal. For the success of Constantine, and not the failure of Albinus, was to be remembered in Britain for many generations. Britain never forgot that she had furnished a world leader and, in seeking to repeat her triumph, she was to waste her strength and ultimately to destroy and dissipate her guardian armies. This tradition, too, was part of Arthur's inheritance.

Later, recognising the need for decentralisation, Constantine rebuilt Byzantium, the ancient city that stood astride the gateway between the eastern and western worlds, and called it Constantinopolis, the City of Constantine, a name which it was to bear proudly for one and a half millenia. From it Rome governed her eastern provinces just as from the Eternal City she governed the western world. When, a hundred years later, Rome herself fell to the barbarians, the city became the repository of Roman power, learning and culture. Here was preserved the Roman inheritance, and from Constantine's city there flowed back, a thousand years later, Roman ideas and Roman knowledge to the new Europe. The renaissance, the rebirth of interest in the ancient world by whose light we still live today, was largely made possible by the work of Constantine, the invader from Britain.

It is to Constantine that Europe also. owes the adoption of Christianity as the religion of the Empire. For Constantine, perhaps influenced by his mother who was a devout Christian, perhaps realising that he could not govern a united Empire if he were to outlaw and to persecute the increasing number of Christian citizens, made Christianity the religion of his government. Before his final victory on the Milvian Bridge outside Rome he claimed to have seen a vision of the cross of Christ. He took as his badge the monogram ☧ , being the first two letters of Christ's name in the Greek alphabet, Chi-Rho, and used it as the ensign of his armies.

Because of the splendour and immensity of his achievements, his name became a magical one in Britain. He and his victorious march to Rome with the legions of Britain were long remembered. The memory was not always accurate, but it dominated the traditions of Britain for many years. It gave to later commanders a belief that they had not only opportunities to seize power, but almost a right to do so. It gave the island a special interest in the Christian faith, and a pride that Britain, through Constantine and his mother Helena, had played a particular part in the foundation of the universal church. Many men died and many armies were lost in pursuing the dream, in later times, that Britain could conquer the world. But through her difficulties and disasters, Britain was sustained and encouraged by the special part she had played in the Christian story. Indeed, since the struggle which Arthur was to lead, of the Britons against the Saxons, was seen by the former as a war of Christian against heathen, it is well to consider how firmly and how anciently rooted was the worship of Christ in Britain.

Even before the days of Constantine, the province had been largely Christian, with priests and bishops, scholars and martyrs, and even her own heretics and heresies. If early traditions are to be believed, at least two churches in Britain were founded within a few decades of the crucifixion, during the lifetime of men who had known Christ or his apostles. Of these two churches, Glastonbury (the better known) is closely linked with the story of Arthur.

The lesser known is the old Parish Church of St Pancras in London, which stands on a patch of rising ground a few hundred yards from the railway station. The present church was built in the nineteenth century, but according to tradition it is on the site of one of the oldest churches in Christendom. The story is shadowy and incapable of proof. The church is said to stand within the boundaries of a Roman camp, of which all traces have vanished. But the camp's outlines and vestiges of the earthen ramparts were visible a couple of hundred years ago. The parish records show that when the church was rebuilt, money had to be spent on carting away several loads of Roman rubble. Tradition says that the older Roman building was a church. The dedication supports this: St Pancras, who was martyred during the persecutions of Diocletian, was the patron saint of the triumph of truth over error, and churches which had fallen into disuse during the period of Saxon heathendom were sometimes rededicated to him. The tradition is further supported by the preservation in the church of an altar stone which though known as St Augustine's stone probably dates from an earlier age.

Another tradition, though slight, could carry the story back into apostolic times. When St Paul was arrested at Jerusalem he claimed his right as a Roman citizen to be tried in Rome. He was sent there by ship, in charge of Julius, a centurion in the 'Band of Augustus'; it has been suggested that the 'Band of Augustus' was the Second Legion, the *Augusta*—the Augustan or Imperial. The evidence is doubtful, for the Vulgate translation of the Bible, made when men were familiar with the Imperial organisation, described Julius as a centurion of the cohort (not the legion) of Augustus. It is at least possible, however, that officers of the Second Legion had been in daily contact with Paul and had from him learned of the new religion. And it is known that among the four legions which served with the Roman army in Britain was the Second; it was part of the force which quelled the rebellion of Boudica. Her final defeat is said to have taken place at Battle Bridge Road, not far from St Pancras Station and near the camp in which St Pancras Church was built, the camp said to be that of the Second Legion. The tumulus on Hampstead Heath some three or four miles away is known locally as 'Boudica's Grave', no doubt a mistaken identification, but stemming from an ancient tradition that she died and was buried close by. If some of the men of the Second Legion were indeed Christians, they may well have set up in their camp in Britain a place of worship; this, disused by Augustine's time, would be the building restored and rededicated to St Pancras.

Better known is the legend of Glastonbury. Here, says tradition, came Joseph of Arimathea who had defied his colleagues in the Sanhedrin by giving Christ a reverent burial after his execution. Unpopular among his own people, in danger from the Roman power which he had also defied, it is possible that Joseph quitted his own land and settled in one of the remoter Provinces. He is said to have brought precious relics: the crown of thorns, from a twig of which he planted the famous thorn tree of Glastonbury; and the cup or dish which Christ used at the Last Supper and in which Joseph is said to have collected some of Christ's blood at the crucifixion. At Glastonbury Joseph is said to have built a small wattle church dedicated to the Virgin Mary, and here with a small company of friends he lived out his days in worship. Traces of this legend can be found in the stories of Arthur: there was the search for the sacred cup, the Holy Grail, by his followers; Arthur himself used an image of the Virgin Mary as a standard; and Galahad, one of the most important of his soldiers, is described by Malory as a descendant of Joseph of Arimathea.

There is no direct early evidence for the Joseph story. His name is not linked with the church until the thirteenth century. Acceptance or rejection of the legend depends upon whether it is taken as a fabrication by dishonest monks or as a written record, however inaccurate, of older stories now lost which had some basis in fact. There is persistent evidence, older than the references to Joseph, of an early association of this site with Christian worship, and of a belief that the foundation of the first church goes back to apostolic times.

Glastonbury is mentioned in one of the Welsh Triads as one of the three places in Britain where choirs sing, by day and by night, the praises of God. Another of the three places is Amesbury, which was destroyed in the sixth century, so that the verse must date back at least to that time. References to fifth-century saints tell us that at Glastonbury they added to and enlarged already existing buildings. This takes us back to a church existing there in the fourth century. William of Malmesbury, writing in the early twelfth century, says: 'There are documents of no small credit, which have been discovered in certain places to the following effect: "No other hands than those of the disciples of Christ erected the church of Glastonbury." Nor is this dissonant from probability.'

He repeats the same tradition when he describes how David, Archbishop of Meneora, who held this place in the late fifth or early sixth century, decided to rededicate the church. David came with seven bishops to perform the ceremony, but during the night while sleeping, 'he beheld the Lord Jesus standing near, and mildly enquiring the cause of his arrival.' On his explaining, the Lord said 'that the Church had already been dedicated by Himself in honour of His Mother, and that the ceremony was not to be profaned by human repetition.' The bishop desisted from his plan and, instead, built another church. William of Malmesbury says that this anecdote is well known and the story and its renown are strong evidence for a very old belief in the immense antiquity of the Glastonbury church and of its dedication to the Virgin Mary.

The original wattle church was still standing in Saxon days; in the earliest Christian times of that epoch, Paulinus, Bishop of Rochester under Augustine, protected it with a covering of planks. The old Church was therefore already ancient then, and some special importance seems to have been attached to it to prompt this act of piety. Moreover, it had one particular quality: it was so sacred that any oath taken by it was peculiarly binding. 'And it is sufficiently evident,' writes William of Malmesbury, 'that, as the men of that province had no oath more frequent, or more sacred, than to swear by the Old Church, fearing the swiftest vengeance on their perjury in this respect.' Other sources provide evidence, as will be seen, that the Roman governors of the fifth and sixth centuries kept, as a matter of business necessity, some sacred relic at their administrative headquarters by which binding oaths could be taken. When later the connection between Arthur and the Grail is considered, this fact and the inviolability of the oaths taken at Glastonbury will have to be examined.

One other reference gives a further hint of Joseph's link with Glastonbury. As pointed out by Geoffrey Ashe in his book *Caesar to Arthur*, one of the Romances dealing with the Holy Cup (a source independent of the monastic writings) says that Joseph is buried 'in the Abbey of Glays'. Although the Romance places Glays in Scotland, this does not destroy the connection, for Patrick, missionary to the Irish, became Abbot of Glastonbury. As a result many Scots from Ireland later went there on pilgrimage, and the name of the place could have become associated with the Scots.

Modern archaeology reinforces legend. During the last few years, Roman pottery which can be dated to the middle of the first century has been dug from the grounds of Glastonbury Abbey. Thus the land hereabouts was occupied, even as the legends tell us, during the lifetime of Joseph and the apostles. But the spade has not yet told us whether this occupation was religious or secular.

Apart from the Glastonbury traditions, there is of course firm archaeological evidence for the existence of Christianity in Roman Britain. At Cirencester was found a square of words scratched on a plaster wall:

R O T A S
O P E R A
T E N E T
A R E P O
S A T O R

The letters can be rearranged to give the words 'Pater Noster' in the form of a cross, together with the letters A and O, the equivalent of the Greek Alpha and Omega, used to denote Christ :

```
                        A
                        P
                        A
                        T
                        E
                        R
        A    PATER  N OSTER    O
                        O
                        S
                        T
                        E
                        R
                        O
```

This word-square has been found in several places, including Pompeii. Since we know the date of the eruption of Vesuvius, the inscription at Pompeii must be dated to within forty years or so of the crucifixion. The Cirencester inscription could therefore be very early.

At the Chedworth villa in Gloucestershire, objects bear the mark of Christ's monogram, ☧ . One of the rooms at the Roman villa at Lullingstone, in Kent, was probably a chapel, the walls bearing painted figures in attitude of prayer, and this sacred monogram. At Silchester, in the Roman town of Calleva Atrebatum, a small building has been excavated that was almost certainly a Christian church. And recently in Canterbury has been found a hoard of Roman silver and gold articles, including coins dating from AD 354 to 423. One of the spoons and an implement bear the Chi-Rho monogram.

Most striking of all is the mosaic in the fourth-century villa at Hinton St Mary, Dorset, discovered in 1963. The main feature

in one of the rooms is a portrait identified by Professor J. C. M.
Toynbee (*Journal of Roman Studies*, Vol. LIV, 1964) as that
of Christ.

There is also some evidence from historians. Constantius, perhaps because of his association with Helena (herself a Christian
from Britain), protected the Christians in his territories from the
destruction which the Emperor Diocletian had planned for them.
Constantius was then Emperor in the West, Lord of Britain and
of Gaul. He was obliged to implement Diocletian's orders but
is said to have done so as mildly as possible. According to Lac-
tantius, 'he did not destroy the temple built up to God in the
hearts of the faithful.' Bede, in the context of this persecution,
refers to Constantius as 'a man of exceptional kindness and
courtesy'. Eusebius writes, though probably mistakenly, that Constantius had Mass celebrated at his Continental headquarters. The
evidence is clear for the existence of a strong body of Christians in Britain, including people of consequence and influence.

Mild though Constantius's policy may have been, Britain's
Christians did not entirely escape the persecution of Diocletian,
Emperor from 284 to 304. Bede tells of some who then suffered.
Most famous is St Alban of Verulamium who, though not yet a
Christian, gave shelter for some days to a priest; he was tortured
and beheaded on the rising ground where St Alban's Cathedral
now stands. Bede gives us the names of two other British martyrs,
Aaron and Julius, and speaks of many others 'of both sexes
throughout the land.'

Some ten years later in 314, we know that three bishops from
Britain attended the Council of Arles in Gaul; the Bishops of
York, London and the *'civitas colonia Londinensium'*—probably an error for Colchester. Britain also produced her own here-
tic, Pelagius, who left his native land about AD 380. In Rome
he had found intolerable the doctrine of total submission to the
will of God, and the concept that salvation did not lie within
man's will but only in divine grace. He thought this destructive

of free will and of the dignity of man. His heresy (which has been called a typically British conception) was the idea that man could be saved by his own merits and good works alone. The heresy spread rapidly in the Near East and was brought back to Britain some forty years later by exiles from Rome. It was to add to the disunity of the Britons and to the difficulty of their struggle against the heathen invaders. It was therefore to be one of the problems which the predecessors of Arthur, if not Arthur himself, had to face as they so stoutly defended Britain's ancient and deep-rooted Christian tradition.

CHI-RHO MONOGRAM WITH ALPHA AND OMEGA

III

THE COMING OF THE KNIGHTS

ROMAN BRITAIN had many frontiers to defend. North of Hadrian's Wall the tribes and clans of Caledonia remained untamed. Their toughness in battle and the inaccessibility of their mountainous country gave them a permanent independence, and the Roman authority was content to look at them defensively rather than aggressively. Over Hadrian's Wall passed carefully controlled trade and traders. The Picts thus saw not only the military power of Rome, the trained bodies of men marching, the plumes, breastplates and forbidding weapons; but also the wealth of the Roman diocese. They saw the silver and gold, the villas with their treasures of bronze and marble, the good money passing in shop and market, all the warmth, sparkle and glitter of the province. These things appeared to them not as a system to emulate but as an abundance to loot once the trumpets were silent and the beacons extinguished.

To the west, the Irish Channel was another frontier; across lay the misty island of Hibernia. Here lived the Scots (who later migrated to Caledonia, giving it their name). They too had seen the treasures of Britain. Only a narrow sea divided them from the warm and comfortable things of the Roman Island. The Second Legion at Exeter and the Twentieth in Chester stood guard but the Scots of Ireland, like the Picts in the North, were waiting. Britain's eastern frontier, then as later, lay on the Rhine river. From the lands around its mouth the curved ships of the

Saxons and their neighbours already threatened. On these eastern and western frontiers, as on the northern, Rome's policy (and the policy of the Roman Island) was purely defensive. The garrison of the Wall, the legions, and the British fleet stood guard.

But pressures there brought about two far-reaching developments. One was the unity which arose between the three hostile folk, the Picts of Caledonia, the Scots of Ireland and the Saxons of Germany. What political or military genius among these people first organised them and persuaded them to work in concert is now unknown. But work together they did, until isolated raids became fused into a full-scale war. The first recorded activity of the Alliance is in 337, when the Picts and Scots are described as raiding Britain together. Five or six years later, the authorities made a treaty with the invaders, and parties of them were settled in Britain. But seven years later the settlers, who were supposed to be defending the island, were raiding the frontier districts in force.

The threat was so great and the numbers so large that the resident garrison was entirely inadequate. A mobile field army from the Continent under Lupicinus, a high-ranking officer, arrived finally to solve the problem; but this hope of a final solution was neither then nor in the future to be fulfilled. For although Lupicinus was successful, within eight years the Barbarian Alliance was massively renewed, with landings from the sea organised to coincide with inland campaigns. Spasmodically it was to last for a hundred years. This Alliance, and not merely the oft-told tale of the coming of the Saxons, contributed largely to the eventual downfall of Britain, and with it Arthur was to contend.

The second development was the expansion of the Roman army; originally this had been an army of Romans, in which only citizens could enlist, and which was essentially a national body. But larger armies than the Roman race could provide became necessary, and there was also a need to harness the energies of the conquered peoples, transforming them from adversaries into partners. Both requirements were answered by enlisting members of other races. Citizenship, no longer a qualification for enrolment, became a reward of service, part of the bounty that went with honourable discharge. The army took men from all the races of the known world. On the tombstones of the soldiers

BADGE OF THE TWENTIETH LEGION, ON A TILE FROM CHESTER

at Chester, used as building material in the city walls, are recorded the birthplaces of many of the soldiers of the Twentieth Legion. From Spain and from Greece, from Gaul and from Asia Minor, the legionaries of Chester stood guard in a strange land.

From the recruitment of individual foreigners, it was a small step to the group recruitment of tribes. Taken from an area where they were actual or potential trouble-makers, a tribe would be enlisted as a complete army unit. They would be moved far from their home, and given land, so that they might defend not only the Roman peace but their own property. Their tribal chief became their regimental commander, with the right to wear the impressive and coveted uniform of a Roman officer. The units so formed were known as *Foederati* or Treaty Troops, their loyalty to Rome being established by a treaty *(foedus)*, under which they received land, pay and equipment in return for military service.

By the middle of the fourth century Constans, son of Constantine the Great, visited Britain and made a treaty with groups of Picts from Caledonia and Scots from Ireland. Some of the Scots seem to have been settled in what is now Wales. Where he settled the Picts we do not know; but no doubt they were planted well south of the Wall—possibly on the western borders. Tribes from western Britain were in turn recruited as *Foederati* and sent to serve on Hadrian's Wall as a defence against the Picts.

Other Treaty Troops were brought over from abroad. For instance, in the last quarter of the fourth century the Emperor Valentinian I brought over a body of Alemanni from the neighbourhood of Mainz in Germany. Their chieftain or king came with them, as commanding officer. This king, Fraomar, was the first Germanic leader in Britain whose name has survived, and so in a sense is the precursor of the English kings. Where he and his followers settled remains unknown. But they were probably used to reinforce the Wall. Fraomar came to Britain some fifty years before that other German leader, Hengist. But he arrived in similar circumstances, as the leader of Treaty Troops and as an ally of the occupying power; his appointment has relevance to the coming of the English.

The population of Britain was taking shape. There were the native Britons, many of them Romanised city-dwellers and villa-dwellers, forming the majority. There were men from all parts of the Empire settled as ex-servicemen round centres like Colchester and Lincoln. There were pockets of barbarians, now admitted as allies, wearing the Roman uniform yet having little understanding of the spirit of Rome. The sword had been given to them, the shield and the eagle; Rome taught them tactics, strategy and organised warfare, the very lessons they needed to learn. Also, they had seen at close quarters the wealth and treasures there for plunder.

This mixed population was the raw material with which every ruler of Britain had to work. Within it, the knowledge that the Roman Island was a political unity—the knowledge that we have seen developing in the independent Emperors of Britain—was set against the tensions and differences between the many races. The individual ex-servicemen, Greeks, Gauls, Levantines or Spaniards, had no difficulties in becoming assimilated into the general life of the island. The Treaty Troops were a different matter; living in groups, they maintained two separate and opposing loyalties—one to the Roman authorities by whose leave they were settled, and one to their own kings and chieftains who still exercised power over them. Some eighty or a hundred years later, Arthur tried to solve this problem by a revival of Roman authority enforced by war.

But the legends of Arthur show him as the leader of mounted men; his battles in the story books are cavalry battles and his companions are knights. We must see how the expanded, multi-racial Roman army changed from massed infantry to mobile cavalry in order to understand how Arthur, the last champion of Roman Britain, came to fight as a cavalryman and not as a legionary commander.

The traditional unit of the Roman army was of course the legion, consisting of about 5,000 infantrymen, armed with spear, sword and shield. Each legion had its auxiliary troops, usually provincials, recruited for their native skill in weapons other than the standard spear and sword. Among these were a few cavalrymen, who might be used as a screen on the flanks, as a skirmishing advance guard or, more usually, to run down and slaughter an already broken enemy.

Rome learned new lessons from the conquered peoples. The Gauls, the Persians, and other nations used mounted men not only in pursuit but in battle. From these were recruited the cavalry wings of the legions and, later, independent mounted units for special duty. By the time of Hadrian, early in the second century AD, in addition to the small cavalry wings attached to the legions, there were in Britain some sixteen independent mounted regiments. One was 1,000 strong, the others 500, giving a total of 8,500 horse. There were other independent auxiliary regiments, many of whom had cavalry squadrons attached, so that already (if we assume the same proportion as with the legions) there were something like 10,000 mounted troops in the island.

When Rome was conquering the world and while she held the initiative, the slow-moving legions could be deployed into victory at will. But when she had to fight defensively along the vast perimeter of the frontiers, she could no longer select the time and place of the engagement; the legions could not march fast or far enough to meet every threat. But in the cavalry Rome had found a shield which she could move swiftly to parry the numerous blows that were falling upon her from so many directions.

So by the fourth century and by the period of the Barbarian Alliance, the cavalryman was well established. He became a common design on coins: a helmeted and cuirassed rider reins in his charger as he spears a fallen barbarian lying beneath his horse's hooves. The same design appears on the tombstones of these mounted soldiers. The legionary was now almost eclipsed. Praise and romance centred on the mounted figure with the spear, the mobile guardian of the Empire: the knight, or a figure very close to the knight, had arrived on the world scene. Long and victorious was to be his career, dominating warfare for at least 1,000 years. It was to be a full 1,000 years before the longbows at Crecy brought him to a pause; and he was not to be finally halted until the coming of gunpowder gave back the glory to the infantryman for a while. Even then he obstinately survived, though he no longer dominated: the last spearman rode out to war in the twentieth century, dressed in the uniform of German *uhlan* and English lancer. Only then did the knight finally dismount, 1,700 years after the Roman bugles first sounded for his saddling.

From the earliest times the Emperors had gathered round themselves a group of companions as counsellors and deputies. These companions *(comites)* could be sent as the Emperor's special representatives wherever local forces required physical or moral reinforcement. To be numbered among them became a high honour, and the word companion *(comes, comitis)* became a designation of rank. These were the officers (whose title we translate as 'count') who played such a vital part in the warfare of the fourth and fifth centuries. One of them, the Count of the Saxon Shore, had been put in charge of Britain's invasion coast; later, as the cavalry arm developed, counts of the various dioceses were appointed: a Count of Spain, a Count of Britain, and others. They were the commanders of mobile field forces and cavalrymen, organised to repel attack and to restore order and the rule of law. They were, in fact, leaders of bands of travelling knights, of knights errant.

Another military designation now began to acquire a territorial significance. The title *dux* originally meant a general officer commanding a large force of legionary troops. Now that the Empire was faced with continued attacks, such officers were stationed permanently in the threatened areas, taking their titles from the territories concerned. There was thus a *Dux Britanniarum*, a Duke of Britain (literally 'Duke of the Britains' since the diocese of Britain was divided into several provinces), who had his headquarters at York. Although his main duties were in the North, he was well placed on the road system to travel swiftly to the south-eastern defences, or south-westwards to Chester and to the legion which stood guard over Wales. The Count of the Saxon Shore had charge of the southern and south-

IV

ARTHUR AS MAXIMUS

TWO young officers serving with Count Theodosius in Britain achieved eminence; and one was to play a disastrous part in the story of the island.

The first was the Count's son, also called Theodosius. The great Count had been murdered by Valens, Emperor in the East. Young Theodosius, still in his thirties, was living quietly in Spain. The long shadows of evening were falling over the Empire. The barbarians were making their final challenge, and in AD 378 Valens himself fell at the battle of Adrianople where the mounted Goths swept aside and destroyed the army of Rome. After this disaster, men remembered the greatness of Count Theodosius and the surviving Emperor, Gratian, summoned young Theodosius from Spain. He was appointed general officer commanding all the cavalry of the Empire and within a few months was made Emperor in the East.

The second young officer, an ambitious and ruthless Spaniard, Magnus Clemens Maximus, also stayed in Britain after the Count's victory over the barbarians. There, when the Picts and Scots again tried to make head against the Roman power, he successfully put them down. But the stage of Britain was too small for his ambitions. Events on the Continent were indeed such as to feed his jealousy. His former colleague was now Emperor, while he himself remained a mere provincial officer. In the West reigned the Emperor Gratian, whom Maximus must have considered far less able than himself, far less suited to wear the purple. And Maximus had the dazzling, to him irresistible, example of Constantine.

In 383, only fourteen years after the terrible invasion of the island, Maximus brushed aside the lesson he should have learned. He was proclaimed Emperor by the army in Britain and sailed for the Continent with all the best troops in the island. The inhabitants of Britain could not remember the dangers of fourteen years earlier but only the sixty-year-old glories of Constantine. Judging by the place of honour which Maximus found in British folklore, he was hailed as a hero and the people of Britain saw themselves for the second time as conquerors of the Roman world.

The British army landed near the mouth of the Rhine, outflanking Gratian's army in northern Gaul. Maximus then brought the armies of Gratian to battle and defeated them. Gratian committed suicide and Maximus thus made good his claim to be Emperor in the West; the title which his armies had bestowed had been confirmed by conquest. He could gaze across Europe towards his former companion in arms, the Emperor Theodosius, with satisfaction. They were once more equals. The two young officers who had campaigned together in Britain now ruled the world.

Later Maximus summoned from the island some of the few remaining troops, in particular those from Hadrian's Wall, which was never again garrisoned. It was now, in 383, that the legions left Britain, not—as has so often been said—in 410 to go to the rescue of Rome. The tale of the army's reluctant departure leaving their friends and families in Britain defenceless, called by duty to save the Eternal City, is not true. It perhaps started with Bede who uses the capture of Rome by the Goths in 410 to date the end of Roman rule in Britain. Although he makes clear in his next chapter that the legions had already been led away 'by rash tyrants' and were never to return, history clings to the sombre and romantic picture of the legions marching to the rescue of Rome.

In fact the legions left jubilant and optimistic, looking forward with grim eagerness to victories on the Continent. Britain had an Emperor again, and under him they would re-create the glories of Constantine. When the reinforcements sailed, leaving the Wall unguarded, they had no sense of doom, thinking to march the road of Empire, and no doubt to return, their standards crowned with laurel.

March the road of Empire they did, but they never saw Britain again. Never again were the castles and signal stations of the Wall to be permanently occupied. Never again did the Roman army fully garrison the Roman Island. Now the beacons were extinguished and the barrack rooms sparsely inhabited, the slow grass began to grow over camp and road, fort and store room. Guard house and stable were never again to hear the gossip of soldiers nor the stamping of the horses. From this date it was not Rome but unaided Britain which had to defend the land as best she might against the barbarian invaders.

When Gratian was defeated, Maximus and his Britons, oppressed by no forebodings, sped from victory to victory. Once more a British army entered Rome to place its leader in the supreme office. Gratian's successor in the West, Valentinian, fled from Rome and obtained refuge with the Emperor Theodosius in the East. So Maximus found himself opposed to his old companion Theodosius and marched against them. This was the road that led Maximus to the walls of Aquileia, on the shores of the Adriatic, to defeat at the hands of the army which Theodosius had raised in the eastern provinces, and to his death.

The dream of Maximus lasted five years. But the adventure of his troops was to last a weary while longer. Tradition relates that, unable or forbidden to return to Britain, they settled perforce on the Continent, and particularly in Armorica on the Atlantic coast of Gaul, which consequently took the name of Brittany. Maximus himself lived on in legend among them. They saw him as a triumphant hero who had conquered Gaul and driven his rival Emperor as a refugee to the East. For five years he had been victorious and borne the title of Emperor. Afterwards the memories of the British survivors did not dwell on the ruin of their hopes or on the defeat of their hero at Aquileia. They remembered their triumph and how through their skill in arms their leader had worn the purple, winning the diadem of the West in the Eternal City. If they remembered Aquileia, they remembered it not as a defeat, but as the climax to their immense endeavour when they, the legions of Britain, marched with all the armies of their leader's dominions—the armies of Gaul, of the Low Countries, and of Spain. They remembered how they had faced the embattled armies of the East from Alexandria, Galatia, Syria, and from all the far lands governed by Theodosius. These exploits they retold in their new home in Brittany.

And echoes of these stories are to be heard in an unexpected context. In the stories of Arthur, who defended Britain 120 years later, are to be found surprising and hitherto unrecognised details of the triumphs and disasters of Maximus.

The troops of Maximus were not the last or only folk from the island to settle in Brittany. Gildas, monk and historian, writing in the middle of the sixth century, tells us that, before the undefended Britons rallied against the waves of invaders, some of them (and this would be about the middle of the fifth century) passed beyond the seas with loud lamentations : 'Thou hast given us as sheep to be slaughtered, and among the Gentiles hast thou dispersed us.' And finally, after Arthur's victories, and after his apparently purposeless and lamentable death in civil war, further waves of refugees left Britain. Their stories, the second layer in the stratified folklore of Brittany, were not of Imperial dreams, as were those of Maximus's veterans. They were of the victories of their dead leader Arthur over invader and heathen, victories which seemed to have been rendered pointless by the tragedy of his death. For with Arthur died the last hopes of Britain and with his passing there faded the last light in the island.

To the descendants of Maximus's soldiers the newcomers told

their story of Arthur's death. The tales of these two separate waves of settlers merged, as stories will that are verbally handed across the generations. By the time the story of Arthur came to be written down in Brittany in the twelfth century or earlier, many of the truths about Maximus appeared as fictions about Arthur. Later English writers made use of the French versions of the story, and repeated these legends. For example, in *Cligès*, a romance written by Chrétien de Troyes in the twelfth century, is a description of preparations made by Arthur for a planned expedition against the East. Arthur, writes Chrétien, summons the great barons of his land, and makes ready galleys, transport and barges. Shields, lances and targets are prepared and armour for his cavalry. Troops were to be gathered from many lands:

> Tote Eingleterre, et tote Flandres,
> Normandie, France, et Bretaigne,
> Et tot desi qu'as porz d'Espaigne . . .

These are not the realms of Arthur. But they are certainly the countries, under their twelfth-century names, which Maximus came to rule, and from which he drew the troops that marched with him to Rome and eastwards to Aquileia.

Even more striking is the list of Maximus's enemies, described as Arthur's enemies, which appears in Malory's *Morte d'Arthur*. Arthur in fact never invaded the Continent nor captured Rome; had he done so, the events would have been firmly recorded, as were the deeds of Maximus and of Alaric. Yet in Malory, as in other later writers, he is recorded as doing so. Again the thread of Arthur is tangled with that of Maximus. Malory tells how the ruler of Rome mustered his forces to oppose Arthur: messengers were sent

> first to Ambage and Arrage, to Alexandrie, to India, to Africa and Europe the large, to Ertayne and Elamya, to Araby, Egypt, and to Damascus, to Damietta and Cayer, to Cappadocia, to Tarsus, Turkey, Pontus and Pamphylia, to Syria and Galatia.

Here surely we are not in fairyland, but before the walls of Aquileia. We are seeing with the eyes of one of Maximus's veterans the battle-line of Theodosius, Emperor in the East, arrayed against us, from far lands we have heard of and from even more distant lands whose names we have not fully comprehended. This list was one of the deep memories of the soldiers and their descendants, and it still stirs us and calls eloquently across the centuries.

Geoffrey of Monmouth, an English historian of the twelfth century, has a similar roll-call in his *History of the British Kings*. He claims to have had access to

> a very ancient book in the British tongue, which, in a continued regular story and elegant style, related the actions of them all, from Brutus the first king of the Britons down to Cadwallader the son of Cadwallo.

Geoffrey's book is a mixture of fact and fancy, but clearly he had seen older records of some kind. His list of the kings of the East who opposed Arthur on the Continent includes the rulers of many of the places in Malory's list; among them are the kings of the Africans, of Egypt and Syria. Other names are different but here is a very similar tradition.

Indeed, the fictional tales of Arthur's invasion of the Continent fit remarkably well the factual deeds of Maximus. In Geoffrey's history, Arthur is visited by an embassy of twelve old men from Rome, bringing a letter from 'Lucius Tiberius', who is described as Procurator of the Commonwealth. Lucius writes that Arthur (whom in this context we may call Maximus-as-Arthur) has offended Rome. He demands the tribute which Britain has paid 'successively from the time of Julius Caesar'. Maximus-as-Arthur is summoned to Rome to be tried by the Senate. Malory tells substantially the same story, except that he describes Lucius not as Procurator but as 'the high and mighty Emperor'.

There is no record of any such demand being made by the central government on Maximus himself. But politically it is just the kind of story which, true or false, he would have told to his troops in Britain to engage their interest and to inflame their loyalty. Told of Arthur, the story is nonsense. Told of Maximus-as-Arthur it is coherent and significant. It gives a glimpse of the prelude to his expedition and of the arguments used to bring unity and purpose to the army. Through the darkness of time and the legends of Arthur, something emerges of the arguments and planning of Maximus.

So in the pages of Malory it is not surprising to find Maximus-as-Arthur invoking the name of Constantine when defying the Roman ambassadors. 'For truly,' he says,

> I will never pay truage to Rome, wherefore I pray you to counsel me. I have understood that Belinus and Brennius, Kings of Britain, have had the empire in their hands many days, and also Constantine the sone of Heleine, which is an open evidence that we owe no tribute to Rome, but of right we that be descended of them have right to claim the title of the Empire.

Geoffrey gives him a very similar speech :

> I . . . now decree that Rome ought to pay tribute to me, because my predecessors formerly held the Government of it. For Belinus the glorious king of the Britons, with the assistance of his brother Brennus, Duke of the Allobroges after they had hanged up twenty noble Romans in the market-place, took their city and kept possession of it for a long time. Likewise Constantine, the sone of Helena and Maximian, who were both my kinsmen, and both wore the crown of Britain, gained the imperial throne of Rome.

Maximian is of course a confused memory of Maximus himself who now, in the shifting kaleidoscope of myth, appears as a further example to, and kinsman of, Maximus-as-Arthur. The Brennius of Malory and the Brennus of Geoffrey are both the historic Brennius the Gaul, who captured Rome in 390 BC. It is not improbable that the historical Maximus, in persuading his troops to follow him, reminded them that Rome itself was not unattainable; not only had Constantine captured it, but so had Brennius in another age. And a mythical or invented British ally of Brennius could well have been mentioned to stir their hearts. Confused memories of barrack-room gossip and of the pre-invasion speeches of generals and staff lie at the root of these stories.

The passages in Geoffrey of Monmouth and Malory describing Arthur's invasion of Europe, which have been taken as invalidating the reliability of both authors, are now seen in a different light. They show that both were recording, accurately though uncritically, genuine traditions containing historical facts about Maximus. This entitles us to assume that once the Maximus-as-Arthur passages are removed, similar truths about Arthur, conveyed by oral tradition over many generations, lie buried in other sections of the texts.

MAXIMUS, FROM A COIN

V

THE ARMY AND THE LAST
REINFORCEMENTS

N OT all Britons were blinded by hero-worship or by the glamour of his capture of Rome to the disastrous results of Maximus's ambition. About 150 years after his death, when the bitter harvest was being reaped, the monk Gildas wrote what he himself describes as the mournful book of Britain's destruction, *De Excidio et Conquestu Britanniae*. On the subject of Maximus his judgment still appears sound.

At length also, new races of tyrants sprang up, in immense numbers, and the island, still bearing its Roman name but casting off her institutes and laws, sent forth among the Gauls that bitter scion of her own planting, Maximus, with a great number of followers, and the ensigns of royalty, which he bore without decency and without lawful right, but in a tyrannical manner, and amid the disturbances of the seditious soldiery. He by cunning arts rather than by valour, attaching to his rule, by perjury and falsehood, all the neighbouring towns and provinces, against the Roman state, extended one of his wings to Spain, the other to Italy, fixed the seat of his unholy government at Trèves, and so furiously pushed his rebellion against his lawful Emperors that he drove one of them out of Rome, and caused the other to terminate his most holy life. Trusting to these successful attempts, he not long after lost his accursed head before the walls of Aquileia, whereas he had before cut off the crowned heads of almost all the world.

After this, Britain is left deprived of all her soldiery and armed bands, of her cruel governors, and of the flower of her youth, who went with Maximus, but never again returned, and utterly ignorant as she was of the art of war, groaned in amazement for many years under the cruelty of two foreign nations—the Scots from the northwest and the Picts from the north.

From AD 388, the date of Maximus's death, can be counted the end of continued Roman rule in Britain. She still looked to Rome both for help and example; but the example faded in the mist of war rolling over the Continent, and help was to be spasmodic.

Seven years after the death of Maximus the Barbarian Alliance again went into action against a Britain now virtually defenceless. The Emperor Theodosius had retired, leaving his eleven-year-old son Honorius as his successor. The reign of Honorius is notable for the prowess of his great general, Stilicho. Like Count Theodosius before him, Stilicho came to Britain and defeated the invaders. His deeds were celebrated by the poet Claudian, who in 399 wrote of Britain's terrible danger, and describes how near she was to death until Stilicho appeared. The Scots were hurling their javelins; but now she was safe and no longer, with tired eyes, must she maintain her vigilance by the coast for the sails of the Saxons. In another poem, Claudian proclaims that with the Saxon defeated, the seas were safer; with the Pict broken, Britain was secure.

Gildas too records the rescue. For immediately after the passage quoted above he writes:

The Britons, impatient at the assaults of the Scots and Picts, their hostilities and dreadful oppressions, send ambassadors to Rome with letters, entreating in piteous terms the assistance of an armed band to protect them, and offering loyal and ready submission to the authority of Rome, if they would only expel the invading forces. A legion is immediately sent, forgetting their past rebellion, and provided sufficiently with arms. When they had crossed over the sea and landed, they came at once to close conflict with their cruel enemies, and slew great numbers of them. All of them were driven beyond the borders, and the humiliated natives rescued from the bloody savagery which awaited them.

But the respite was temporary. In 402 Stilicho needed all his troops to combat the insolent Goths who were again attacking in Europe; he took back, wrote Claudian, his soldiers that had fought in Britain. Gildas also writes of the rescuing legion's departure, leaving Britain to face new invasions and new disasters. The fifth century opened for Britain with growing peril and foreboding.

Militarily weak, her cities decayed, her provinces patrolled by unreliable Treaty Troops and with the shield of Hadrian's Wall broken, she yet had certain advantages. From the deadly inroads of the Franks and Goths, at whose hands her sister dioceses on the Continent were suffering, she was protected by her seas and by the forts along the Saxon Shore. Her agriculture remained reasonably prosperous, and she had excellent roads to give her remaining troops mobility. The walled towns stood ready to be regarrisoned. Here was an adequate foundation upon which a resolute government might well have built.

But Britain, regardless that the time had come to look to her defences, to seek a new and safer destiny within her own shores away from the disintegrating Continent, once more dreamed her dream of Imperial ambition—a dream that was to turn nightmare before she awakened.

Recalling her previous prosperity and independence, she again sought salvation through her own Emperor. In 406 two, Marcus and Gratian, were set up successively, each being swiftly murdered. In the following year, at the Roman city of Calleva Atrebatum, whose grey walls today enclose a few acres of farmland at the village of Silchester in Berkshire, the soldiers gathered once more to proclaim an Emperor, a Lord of Britain. The new man was one of their own number, a private, with no skill or reputation : he was chosen for the extraordinary reason that his name was Constantine.

His full name was in fact Flavius Claudius Constantine; Flavius was one of the names of the great Emperor, and almost certainly the new one adopted it after his elevation; he also gave his son the name of the great Emperor's son, Constans. And he

is said after his elevation to have married a lady descended from
a noble Roman family.

The central government in Rome was in no position to curb
him after his illegal assumption of power and Honorius granted
him recognition. This again demonstrated that the formal offices
of the Empire could in emergency be locally filled. According
to Geoffrey of Monmouth, the new Constantine was Arthur's
grandfather. The dates, as will be seen, put the accuracy of this
story in doubt. Even if he were not Arthur's ancestor, however,
he was certainly one of his political predecessors. In the times
ahead, when all communication with Rome was lost, Britain had
a precedent for the creation of a Count or a Duke of Britain.

Constantine III (as, after his recognition by Honorius, he may
be called) saw his new dignity not as an opportunity for saving
Britain; rather he saw himself as a second and more successful
Maximus. Like Maximus, he crossed over to the Continent, taking the last poor remnant of the trained regular soldiers from the
island. They marched to the frontier of the Rhine and secured it;
they occupied Gaul. They saw the high Pyrenees, and marched
over the passes into Spain, following the footsteps of Maximus.
Perhaps they saw themselves as the saviours of the Empire. The
Rhine was the ancient and traditional frontier, and they watered
their horses there. Spain was one of the oldest provinces, conquered in the legendary days of the Republic, and they secured it.

But the people of Britain shared neither in the glamour of the
adventure, nor in the illusion of success. Only civilians, and
Treaty Troops who were at heart barbarians, remained to
oppose any barbarian attack. Those in authority gathered together, and agreed upon action. They repudiated Constantine
III, removing the deputies he had left in charge. Next, they
organised the first truly British army since the Roman occupation. It was made up of men from many races: Britons, descendants of the legionaries from all the lands of the Empire, Treaty
Troops, Alemanni, Franks, Scots, and many others. Though containing within itself the seeds of internal quarrels and of civil

war, this mixed force was Britain's first national army, and for long it served her well. Finally, to show that they were not rebelling against Rome (who might yet be able to provide help), the Britons wrote to the Emperor Honorius assuring him of their loyalty.

Honorius could not spare troops. The preoccupations of his government on the Continent were many. The Goths, under Alaric, were advancing against Rome itself; Stilicho, his great general who had once rescued Britain, was dead. Nevertheless, Honorius did not ignore the Britons' note. They, in sending it, covered themselves against the time of Rome's possible resurgence; he, in replying, was careful to keep open the possibility of Rome's return to the island.

So a little while before Rome fell to the Goths and the fabric of Roman Europe shattered into the fragments that were to become the modern kingdoms and republics, Honorius sent his reply. Zosimus, an historian who was writing less than 100 years after the events, tells us

> And Honorius, having written letters to the cities in Britain, exhorting them to look to their own safety, and having gained the goodwill of the soldiers by making gifts to them out of the money sent by Heraclian, lived in all ease.

The year was AD 410. Rome, dying, was still able to avenge herself on Constantine III. She sent an army against him and he was killed in battle. In the same year Alaric captured Rome. For the first time for over 800 years, she was taken by a foreign army whose aim was not to seize but to destroy her power.

Despite the stories told, Britain sent no legions to Rome's succour; she had none to send. Her only army now was the new untried force: not the army in Britain, but the British army, whose self-imposed and urgent task was to defend the island, not Rome.

The Gaulish record known as the *Chronicle of Prosper Tiro*, which was probably written at the time of the events described, makes it clear that the barbarians were quick to realise their opportunities; for in 410 'Britain was devastated by an incursion of Saxons.' Zosimus, however, says that 'the Britons, taking up arms, and struggling bravely on their own behalf, freed their communities from the onslaught of the barbarians.' Procopius, writing about a century later, reports:

> Constantine was defeated in battle and slain, together with his sons. Notwithstanding this, the Romans were never able to recover Britain, which thenceforth continued to be ruled by usurpers.

His use of the word 'usurpers' and not 'barbarians' indicates that in his day (the middle of the sixth century), Britain still had rulers who held power by usurpation and not by conquest; they adopted or usurped Roman titles and were not mere barbarian chiefs. True, Prosper Tiro claims that in 441 Britain was 'reduced to subjection by the Saxons', but as at this date the main Saxon immigration had not taken place, that is exaggeration. She was suffering from Saxon and other barbarian attacks, but the British army was still fighting back.

For Britain the outstanding fact of the year 410 was not the fall of Rome, but the first defence of Britain by the Britons. The long years of Roman rule, the experiments of independence under Carausius and Allectus, and the success of Constantine, had changed the island from a group of separate and scattered tribes into a land that saw itself as a unity, first political and now military. The nation-state was coming to birth. Whether the new Britain was to be inhabited by the old mixed population, or by the German tribes, or to be divided between both, was still to be decided. The new British army was the instrument with which Arthur made possible a fourth solution—the preservation of part of the old population in sufficient numbers to ensure that they stayed obstinately in their island, to fight and to merge with the German invaders, so that a people would arise who were a fusion of both but identical with neither.

The repudiation by Britain of Constantine III and the note to Honorius set powerful precedents. Both actions demonstrated that the municipalities and States of Britain could hold a unified policy even after the Roman administration that had bound them together had crumbled away; and that local Britons, whether native or descendants of Romans, could take and hold office with the force of law; and that Britain could organise her own defences and herself make head against the invaders. Arthur was to follow all these precedents.

THE LONDON MEDAL OF CONSTANTIUS CHLORUS

Gildas the monk died in AD 570, so that his book was written less than 150 years after the events just described; his evidence on Britain's situation must be carefully examined.

After noting the career of Maximus, he mentions the coming of a legion to rescue the Britons from further attacks of the Scots and Picts. This sounds like the campaign of Stilicho although he does not mention Stilicho by name. Doubts have been cast upon Gildas's evidence for this period, because he describes the building of

a wall across the island, from one sea to the other, which being manned by a proper force, might be a terror to the foes whom it was intended to repel, and a protection to their friends whom it covered. But this wall, being built of turf instead of stone, was of no use to the foolish people who had no head to guide them.

The turf wall in the North, from sea to sea, was built nearly 300 years earlier, and undoubtedly Gildas had grasped the wrong end of the stick; but the stick existed. No doubt Stilicho did take steps to improve the defences of Britain; at one of the forts of the Saxon Shore, Pevensey, tiles have been found stamped with the name Honorius. Gildas is recording inaccurately as to place, but accurately as to the event, that Stilicho came with troops, cleared large areas of Britain of invaders and built or repaired the defences.

On the shadow emperor, Constantine III, Gildas is silent. But after his account of Maximus, he tells of renewed atacks by the barbarians and later of Rome again sending Britain some troops, this time described as a combined force of sailors and cavalry. They came in response to an abject appeal; its terms suggest that it was made by a Britain separated from the Empire, that is to say after the fall of Constantine III and the organisation of independent defences. That there is no evidence of this second rescue from any other writer does not disprove Gildas's story. On the Continent men's minds were preoccupied with other tragedies and nearer events. Perhaps some military leader in Gaul, concerned with defending his northern flank rather than with helping the Britons, took the initiative.

He must have come a few years after 410 (that is after Constantine III's death and the exchange of notes between the Britons and Honorius), but before 429, since we have a witness for that year who came to Britain and found no Roman troops. The memory of this expedition handed on to Gildas was of a swift-moving cavalry force rolling back the invaders. The horsemen came like eagles in their flight: their victorious swords smote the shoulders of their foes; the enemy fell like leaves in autumn; the cavalry surged forward like a mountain torrent in flood, sweeping all before it. It is a record not of a long and bitter campaign but of a swift and bloody vengeance. It provided for the Britons yet another proof of the invincible power of the armoured horsemen against the barbarians.

These fifth-century horsemen possessed two advantages unknown in the period of Rome's greatness: the stirrup and chain mail. Before the stirrup came, the horse was a vehicle that could carry a man. After, it became a moving base from which a man could fight. The Goths used the stirrup and Rome had learned the terrible lesson of Adrianople, where a whole army of their infantrymen had been destroyed by Gothic horsemen who fought as they rode. Chain mail, known for many years as an adjunct to plate armour, was now made large enough to cover a man's body. The horseman became almost invulnerable while his own mobility was unimpaired. These mail-clad riders, or *cataphracti*, rode in independent detachments and were able to break the stubbornest of foes.

So Gildas's words come to life. Such men would indeed be a gale of death blowing through the countryside, bringing down the enemy like autumn leaves. Gildas adds that the rescuing expedition 'vigorously drive our enemies' band beyond the sea, if any could so escape them. For it was beyond those same seas that they had transported, year after year, the plunder which they gained, no one daring to resist them.' So the main enemies were not the Picts from Caledonia nor the Scots settled in the West, but seaborne invaders from the Continent. Gildas adds that Britain was being invaded not only by the Picts and Scots, but by those who came by sail and by oar. Invincible on the sea, these invaders were beaten on the land by the *cataphracti*, and only a remnant returned home, licking their wounds, mourning their dead, and discouraged from further raids for a few years. The Saxons were not yet coming as permanent settlers, but as raiders returning at the end of each year's expedition, carrying away their loot.

Gildas records that before the Roman force returned to the

Continent 'they then give energetic counsel to the timorous natives, and leave them patterns to manufacture arms.' Also, the Britons were told that the Romans would not again send troops. By subduing the enemies of Britain and by teaching the Britons to make arms, the Roman commander, a realist, was seeking to establish an effective ally to cover his northern flank; his action is a translation into military and practical terms of the note of Honorius 'to the States of Britain, exhorting them to look to their own safety'.

Gildas writes that the leaders of this expedition 'built a wall different from the former, by public and private contribution, and of the same structure as walls generally, extending in a straight line from sea to sea.' This again is a description of Hadrian's Wall, built 300 years earlier. But Gildas could be recalling a tradition that once more the commander of the expedition had seen to the repair of some of Britain's defence works. He adds:

> Moreover, on the south coast where their vessels lay, as there was some apprehension lest the barbarians might land, they erected towers at stated intervals, commanding a prospect of the sea.

It is not true that a series of watch towers was built along the Saxon Shore at this late date, but there may well have been renovation, reorganisation and reoccupation.

This Commander of the Third Rescue was seeking no conquest and stayed maybe for a few months only. He was, as it were, the proto-Arthur, a man who used the same weapons and the same kind of plan that Arthur was to pit against the same enemies in the years that followed. His name is unknown, and his very existence lies in the doubtful areas of legend; yet it was under his guidance that the new-formed British army fought its first successful campaign. And it was his troops who gave substance and reality to the frail words of Honorius. Arthur must have known of these events in the same way as they were known to his contemporary Gildas. Whether the latter's account is accurate or not, it represents the story current in Arthur's Britain and Arthur would have believed and learned much from it.

The cavalry re-embarked, the horses clattering up the gang-planks, the victorious soldiers relaxed in the ships taking them to new battles and new adventures. Sails were hoisted and oars dipped. As their commander saw the grey walls of the harbour town, banded with red brick, merge into mist, there snapped Britain's last military link with the Continental armies of Rome. To the anxious eyes watching from the British coast, the war-ships and transports faded into the far horizon. Never again would legate or tribune, Roman cavalryman or rescuing com-mander, sail back across those grey waters from Roman Europe. Military reinforcements there might be again, but these would be from the kinglets and chieftains who were the local and partial successors of the crumbling world state. Rome as a mili-tary power had vanished out of Britain. The shadowy figure of proto-Arthur is a symbol of finality.

Yet Rome, her armies scattered and her dominions fallen away, found a new organisation through which her influence could continue. The officers she sent no longer wore the helmets of commanders and were no longer legates of a legion: they wore the mitres of bishops, and were the legates of the new ecclesiastical power. They carried the same message of discipline, of service and unity—the message of a single community in Europe, now united not by the eagles but by the badge of Christ.

The distinction between the civilised and the barbarian took on a new meaning. It was no longer the distinction between those living within and without the geographical limits of the Empire, but the distinction between those who were members of the Christian community and those who were heathen or pagan. The struggle of the Romanised inhabitants of the old Empire against the barbarians became a war between Christians and heathens.

Rome remained the Eternal City and through her new instrument, the Church, remained the acknowledged head of the Christian world. Among the titles borne by the Emperors of Rome had been that of *Pontifex Maximus*, or chief priest of the state religion. This title the Bishops of Rome inherited, and with it some of the authority of the Emperors; Bishop of Rome, chief priest of the Christian community, God's deputy, and Father (or Pope) of the Church, were significant titles. And since he who bore them sat in Rome, they carried an authority which men had been accustomed to accept for 400 years. Though Rome's military weapon was broken, she had meanwhile forged another almost as potent and certainly more enduring.

If the Christian faith was to serve as a unifying force, it had to be unified in itself. Rome could no more permit conflicting beliefs within the Christian community than in earlier days she could permit local army commanders to develop independent policies. During the fourth and fifth centuries the Church was stamping out heresies and imposing unity of belief.

Germanus, the recently appointed Bishop of Auxerre in Gaul and formerly a soldier, was sent by the Church in 429 to retrieve the Britons from the then flourishing heresy of Pelagius, described in Chapter II. He found the Britons living a fairly normal life, governed by local kings, and their towns at least in part maintained. His biography, written about fifty years later, shows that although the Picts and Scots were raiding and the Saxons had made landings the situation was still far from disastrous. Germanus can refer to Britain as 'that most wealthy island'. His visit alone—it was repeated eighteen years later—shows that communications were still open between the island and Gaul, and that the British army was not altogether unsuccessful.

During the spring of 429 some of the Picts and Scots renewed their alliance with parties of Saxons and were harrying the countryside; the leaders of the British army appealed to Germanus for help. He gave them both spiritual and military succour. In the camp he built a temporary wooden church, in which to celebrate Easter, and there he baptized such of the Britons as were not already Christians. He also took personal command of the army.

Germanus's soldiers were not fully equipped and the enemy advanced on the camp expecting an easy victory. But Germanus was ready for them, concealing his troops in the steep hills surrounding the valley in the line of the enemy's advance; behind bush and boulder, the Britons silently awaited the marauders as they approached, fording the river and advancing up the apparently deserted valley. When they stood within the encircling hills, Germanus sprung his trap. Rising from cover, and bearing the standard of the army in his own hands, he and his fellow priests gave the pre-arranged signal, a triple shout of 'Alleluia!' The call was taken up by the British army, who roared their triumphant battle-cry across the valley. Fearing imminent encirclement the barbarians turned and ran; the retreat became a rout. The river had been a simple obstacle when advancing, but it made orderly retreat impossible. Many flung aside their arms in order to swim across; many drowned, and the British victory was complete.

The Alleluia victory of 429 was a landmark, as for the first time the defence of Britain took on the nature of a crusade. A priest bore the standard, and 'Alleluia' was the call. The Britons were fighting not only for their island, but for the right to remain within the Christian community. Here another precedent was set for Arthur, who seized on it and closely identified the British with the Christian cause. His standard was not the Eagle but the Cross, and he carried not the image of an Emperor but of the Virgin Mary.

The battle demonstrated that the British Army lacked only leadership. The biographer of Germanus mentions neither count nor duke, but only an army of soldiers, disciplined enough to follow a plan but lacking a general. It also showed that the examples of Count Theodosius, Stilicho and the Commander of the Third Rescue had been overlooked. The British had no cavalry with which to exploit their tactical advantage, turning the rout into slaughter.

Arthur was born some fifty or sixty years after this battle. He could have spoken with men whose fathers fought in it. He could study its details and the lessons it taught.

VI

THE LAST TREATY TROOPS

WHEN the Romans first came, Britain was inhabited by numerous tribes, each with its own well-defined territory ruled by its king or queen. These tribal areas were independent and often mutually hostile. Their civilisations varied and their policies, when confronted with the Romans, varied also. Some welcomed the invaders while others fought them bitterly. Rome ultimately forced a unity upon them which outlasted Roman rule itself.

The tribal areas had their capitals, which the Romans called *oppida*. The Romans seized upon these as evidence that the Britons had a rudimentary knowledge of city life, and reorganised them on Roman lines, rebuilding them with forum temples and baths, and with a meeting place for the council. This council was a local version of the Senate in Rome with elected officers and magistrates. The new Romanised towns were called *civitates*, and the name came to mean not only the towns themselves but the whole tribal areas.

These *civitates*, or States of Britain, retained their identity throughout the Roman period and after. They ensured that the tribal royal families found a place in the new order. The kings sat in the local Senate, adding their prestige to the assembly, and fortifying their own authority from it. Their sons and grandsons continued the tradition. Thus when Britain was left isolated in the fifth century and when Roman officials were withdrawn, the old royal families could resume their tradition of authority, and the States of Britain continued to function.

The Romans taught the States of Britain to send delegates to an annual Provincial Council. This met at Camulodunum (Colchester) and when the Romans vanished, the habit remained. For the States of Britain seem to have continued to act in concert. It was they who had sent the note to Honorius; it was to them that Honorius had replied. It was they, still acting in unison, who had sought the help that came with the commander of the last reinforcements. They retained this unity of purpose, perhaps tenuous but nonetheless real, for another 100 years.

After AD 410, the States of Britain were reverting to their old monarchies, but retaining many of the forms of government taught by the Romans. Prefects and tribunes were appointed and the old Roman offices, with differences, survived. These revived kingdoms continued for a century or more, and Gildas lists no fewer than five in his day, towards the middle of the fifth century. To Continental observers, steeped in Roman tradition, these local kings with their assumed Roman titles were, as Procopius alleged in the account quoted in the last chapter, 'usurpers' indeed; but this form of usurpation showed a desire for continuity. Its survival into the sixth century emphasises the slowness of the Saxon conquest. For seventeen years after the Alleluia victory the patchwork of Britain's defences—her own army, Treaty Troops, the local levies of the States of Britain—seems to have stood firm.

The forts still stood along the invasion coast and were to stand a great while longer. From them the army of Britain could guard the coast and ensure that few landings were unopposed, few piracies unavenged. Faintly, perhaps, we see persisting the work of the last Roman commander. Peril finally came not from the terrible curved ships of the Saxons; indeed, as the Saxons later came to be regarded by the Britons as potential allies, they could not then have been active partners in the Barbarian Alliance. It came from the Picts in the North, where the Wall lay open, and from the Scots in the defenceless West. In 446 the attacks of these two groups were more than Britain could repel. The States of Britain met to find a solution.

According to Gildas, this was done by 'a pitiful remnant'. In the light of Britain's long resistance thereafter this cannot be taken literally. A clue to his meaning lies in the words of Nennius who says that at that time the king (or perhaps the dominant king) of Britain was motivated by fear not only of the Picts and Scots, but also of the Romans and in particular Ambrosius. Here is a glimpse of two major parties in Britain: the pro-Roman party led by Ambrosius who still hoped for a revival of Roman rule; and their opponents who were convinced that the Roman power had vanished forever. It was this latter group which consulted together. In the view of the pro-Roman Gildas they would represent but a remnant of Britain, and, in the light of the disastrous results of their policy, would have indeed appeared pitiful.

Ambrosius is said to have been a son of the King of Damnonia, that is of the modern Devon and Cornwall. His name suggests that he was Roman by descent, or born of a Romanised family. Some of the stories make Arthur his kinsman, others his lieutenant. In either case we have here a hint of Arthur's origins somewhere in Cornwall. Ambrosius was to fight bravely against the barbarians when the need came, but at present he stood aloof.

The leader of the group that met together was called Guorthigirnus by Nennius, and Gurthrigernus by Gildas. A Roman would have called him Vorthigernus or Vurthrigernus, and he is known to history as Vortigern. Nennius traces back his descent through many generations of kings. Therefore he was a member of one of the native princely houses which had resumed kingship when Roman rule ended. He had no interest in seeing the revival of Roman rule which would have meant the end of his royal power, but he had a strong motive to defend his own kingdom. This lay probably in North Wales, but his authority extended to the southeast of the island, and he had become the leading king in Britain. Nennius dates Vortigern's reign as beginning 'when Valentinian, son of Placida, was Consul' and also 'when Theodosius and Valentinian were Consuls'. This means that it opened in AD 425-6.

Under his leadership, the States of Britain (or Gildas's 'remnant' of them) appealed once more to Rome for reinforcements. It was hoped perhaps that the rescue would be effected by a visiting force which would have no effect upon the internal affairs of the island. Rome was in no position to re-establish her permanent rule to the detriment of the new kings; to seek her help now seemed safe. We know the date of this appeal, because Gildas tells us that it was sent to Aetius (he mis-spells it Agtius), 'Consul for the third time', and the third consulship of Aetius was in 446. As it was sent in the name of the Britons, the Provincial Councils appear still to have been functioning and the States of Britain, or some group of them, were still acting in unison.

Gildas records part of the text of the Note that was sent to Rome. It is worth recalling in the original Latin, these the last formally recorded words of the States of Britain :

> Agtio ter consuli gemitus Britannorum. . . . Repullunt nos barbari ad mare, repellit nos mare ad barbaros; inter haec oriuntur duo genera funerum, aut jugulamur, aut mergimur.

> To Aetius, Consul for the third time, the groans of the Britons. . . . The barbarians drive us into the sea, and the sea drives us against the barbarians. Between these, two kinds of death happen to us; either we are slaughtered, or we are drowned.

So Britain was standing with her back to the sea trying to fight off the inland barbarians who had overrun the country. The sea was her only refuge, a fatal one for in it her people would drown. We have the picture of a land in turmoil, but not of any inroads by the seafaring Saxons.

Rome could not help. When the bleak news came back to Britain, it chilled men's hearts. Only now was it fully realised that the eagles would never again lead the citizens (as the Britons still called themselves) against the barbarians. The Eternal City had reached the end of her story. Even her fall to the Goths, a young man's lifetime away, had not seemed so numbing. From her fall she could recover, and help might be—and was—again sent. But now the end had come.

Divided, ruled by many kings, faced by the determined barbarians, with her back to a hostile and lonely ocean, over which she could never again expect to see the rescuing warships coming out of the grey mist, as triumphantly as the sound of a bugle in a morning's silence, desperate and with all her resources stretched, Britain stood at bay.

Again a council was held to discuss means of holding back the Picts and Scots. Vortigern presided, and in this context Gildas refers to him by the Roman title of 'dux'. The predominant king, he had either assumed, or was thought to have assumed, the formal designation of the military leader—Duke of Britain. Geoffrey of Monmouth refers to him as Consul of the Gewissans, which again suggests the survival of Roman designations.

Vortigern and his council remembered the old practice of establishing Treaty Troops. The Alliance between the Picts and the Scots was now too firm for either of those nations to enlist. There was, however, a third possibility—the Saxons. They were known to be effective soldiers and some of them or their near relations had already served and settled in Britain. A treaty with them would involve the grant to them of British land, and if this land were given in the South East, they could be relied upon to fight off any intruders from overseas.

The council duly chose the small island of Thanet, good farmland, attractive to the settlers, and cut off from the mainland by a wide channel dominated by the largest of the Saxon forts, Portus Rutupiae. The walls of this fort still stand at Richborough and we can see what an impregnable place it was. Locked in by this channel, guarded by the grey walls and watchtowers of Portus Rutupiae and by the sister fort of Regulbium to the north, the Saxon Treaty Troops were not to be admitted into Britain proper except when on active service with her army.

Careful planning lay behind the bringing in of this new body of allies. The States of Britain were acting not in panic, but in accordance with sound Roman precedent. They had learned the lesson which Rome had taught of consultation and unity. Vortigern's titles of *dux* or *consul* show that some of the old military organisation survived; the Roman Island was still functioning in the Roman manner. But the solution she sought, though apparently wise, proved disastrous. The settlers in Thanet were the last Treaty Troops to be enlisted in the army of Britain, and the stage was now set for a long and bitter war.

The accepted date for the settlement of the Saxon Treaty

THE ISLE OF THANET

Troops is 447. Nennius gives the names of their chieftains as Hengist and Horsa. Hengist, their leader, was probably their commanding officer when they enrolled in the army of Britain.

Their numbers at first were not large. Gildas says they came in three ships and this probably means no more than 200-300 men. Gildas used the Saxon word *keels* for their ships, but his British tongue stumbled over the outlandish expression and he spelt it *cyulae*. So the first English word to be recorded in Britain is a seafaring word. These three vessels were the first of many which were to carry the English people to Britain and thence to other lands. Westwards to America, southwards to Australia, eastwards into Asia, and along the shimmering coasts of Africa, the English ships were later to make landfall; until the strange language, in which the hoarse commands were shouted to bring those three keels ashore on Thanet, encircled the round globe.

They landed, says Gildas, claiming that they were to fight for Britain against her enemies. Reinforcements came from Germany to join them; they were introduced as soldiers, to undergo great dangers on behalf of the Britons. They were granted regular supplies, and these grants continued peacefully for a long time. Gildas knew the tragic ending of the story and his account is coloured by his foreknowledge. The Saxons are the whelps of lions; they are dogs and bastards and worse. But his rhetoric does not hide the fact that here was an orderly settlement of Treaty Troops with the consent of the authorities.

Nennius adds that Vortigern received the Saxons as friends. Like Gildas he notes that they came in three keels, but in his narrative Hengist and Horsa are described as exiles from Germany. Nennius reports that in the same year Germanus, the victor of the Alleluia battle, paid a second visit to Britain. This is confirmed by a biography of Germanus, written independently. This time the soldier-bishop fought no battles but carried on his pastoral mission 'undisturbed by war'. Here is evidence that the raids of the Picts and Scots had not destroyed ordered life in Britain; and that the Saxon Treaty Troops were still a protection and not a threat.

Witnesses from the Saxons now appear, to supplement British sources. For, after they had conquered, they wrote their story in the form of a brief summary of events for each year, the *Anglo-Saxon Chronicle*. The entries for these early years give us the Saxons' own traditions, and provide a means of checking the evidence of the British writers. The coming of the Saxons is entered under the year 447, but is not ascribed to that precise date. Hengist and Horsa, we are told, came at the invitation of Wurtgern, King of Britain, who instructed them to fight against the Picts. (There is no mention of the Scots.) They were everywhere successful and after these first victories sent messages back to Germany for reinforcements. The *Anglo-Saxon Chronicle* adds one detail not mentioned by Gildas: the Saxons sent the message to another tribe, the Angles, who lived to the north of the Saxons in Germany. They arrived with another neighbouring tribe, the Jutes. It was the Angles who finally gave their name to the country of Angleland or England and we may now, in anticipation of the unification of these tribes, begin to speak of the English.

For some eight years the Treaty Troops lived in Thanet, defending the Britons, and building up their own numbers legally and peaceably. The pro-Roman party of Ambrosius, who had taken no part in Vortigern's establishment of this new settlement, seemed to be discredited. But as the numbers of the settlers increased it became clear that the Isle of Thanet could not provide sufficient land. Nennius tells a romantic story of King Vortigern's falling in love with Hengist's beautiful daughter. In return for the hand of his daughter, Hengist was granted the whole kingdom of Kent. This story is mentioned neither by the *Anglo-Saxon Chronicle* nor by Gildas, but it is credible: Vortigern's kingdom had been secured by the military skill of his new allies, so that to extend their territory and to confirm the alliance by a dynastic marriage would have appeared sensible. But because the result proved disastrous, the marriage was seen by the Britons of a generation later as a betrayal. Evil and lustful motives were ascribed to Vortigern, who is said by Nennius to have been instigated by the devil. But at the time, the marriage as well as the extension of the territory of the Treaty Troops must have appeared prudent and sensible.

That the settlement of Kent was peaceful and arranged with the permission of the British authorities is borne out by the survival of the name of that kingdom in the new land of England. The names of most of the other States of Britain and of their peoples have not survived. The territory of the Iceni became the kingdom of the East Saxons, and survives as the county of Essex; the kingdom of the Trinovanti became the dwelling of the

South Folk, and the memory of the Trinovanti has perished from
the county of Suffolk. But because the Treaty Troops were peacefully given the territory of the Cantii, they held it by its old
name, and it remains the county of Kent to this day. When they
later built their own capital town there the English did not give
it a new name, for the people whose land they had been granted
still dwelt there. They called it the borough of the Cantii,
Cantware burg, and the name Canterbury too survives.

During the negotiations described by Nennius, Hengist talked
with Vortigern through an interpreter named Ceretic. This is
clearly a British name, the same as that borne by the British
hero Caractacus 400 years before. The Caractacus of Claudius's
time, which is the Caradoc of modern Wales, had now become
Ceretic, the intermediate form before the name is met again as
Cerdic. And the mere fact that the Saxons were employing Britons
as interpreters and assistants is further evidence that the two
peoples were beginning to associate.

But this peaceful state of affairs did not last. Gildas, Nennius
and the *Anglo-Saxon Chronicle* alike tell of the revolt of the last
Treaty Troops. Gildas reports that the English picked a quarrel
on the grounds that their monthly allowance was insufficient;
Nennius tells us that the Britons tried to end the grants of food
and clothing because the numbers of the English had greatly
increased whilst the need for their services had ended. The stories
are not contradictory. After several victories over the Picts, and
having brought reinforcements from Germany with the approval
of the Britons, the English had found their military duties less,
which increased their interest in acquiring land for peaceful farm-
ing. The Britons had found it unreasonable to continue pay and
supplies when the need for active allies had diminished. The
Treaty Troops had served their purpose.

Through interpreters, and with many misunderstandings,
negotiations had taken place, Vortigern suggesting that the Saxons
could have more land, which they could defend when need arose.
But they would no longer be part of the army; pay and supplies

would have to be reduced or to cease. The marriage of Hengist's daughter to Vortigern had probably sealed the agreement made. Kent or some part of it was, as already seen, granted to the English. This was done at the cost of British unity, for Nennius comments that the arrangement was made behind the back of the ruler of the Cantii.

There were now clear causes for misgivings among the Britons. With the Treaty Troops only sullenly accepting the new situation, and with the native ruler of the Cantii smouldering with resentment at the betrayal of his territory, the conflicting forces in the army of Britain began to be revealed. Many of Vortigern's own followers may have felt that their leader's policy was proving disastrous and that the policy of the pro-Roman party of Ambrosius in the West had been vindicated. Vortigern, with an unsettled and almost rebellious ally to his south-east, and with a critical and watchful group of pro-Roman States to his west, was in danger. It was essential that he should become reconciled to Ambrosius and reunite the States of Britain so that, should his formidable English allies make further demands or attempt a mutiny, the army of Britain would be united to oppose them.

This is exactly what Nennius, though in the language of myth, tells us that he did. The story deals with the birth of a son begotten incestuously by Vortigern upon his own daughter, but clearly tells of the political steps which Vortigern took.

For his many sins he was rebuked by the clergy of Britain. Immediately afterwards, he called a council of his advisers who pointed out the danger that was threatening from the Saxons. They advised the King to go to the remoter parts of his kingdom, and to build a citadel. Vortigern travelled to the West and was advised by his counsellors that he should 'find a child born without a father, put him to death and sprinkle with his blood the ground on which the citadel is to be built, or you will never accomplish your purpose.' He sent officers throughout Britain to look for such a boy.

One was found and taken before Vortigern so that his blood could be sprinkled over the ground. But the boy, by magic, challenged the King's counsellors. He revealed that beneath them was a pool, and in the pool two vases. These were dug up, and in one the boy showed that there was a tent; and in the tent two sleeping dragons, one red and one white. The dragons then fought with one another. Three times the white dragon overcame the red, but finally the red dragon drove the white through the pool and it disappeared. The boy said that the red dragon was the dragon of Britain, and the white was the dragon of the Saxons. Just as the red dragon had prevailed, so the people of Britain would drive the English people over the seas, back to their own land. He forbade the King to build his city on that spot, saying that it was his and he would remain there. Asked his name, the boy said 'I am called Ambrosius.' (Nennius also gives the British form of the name, Embries Guletic, or Prince Ambrose.) 'My father is one of the consuls of the Romanised people.' Vortigern, his mission unsuccessful, left Ambrosius in possession of the spot, and built his citadel elsewhere.

The symbolism of the dragons, the need for human sacrifice before a city can be built, and the contradiction of the fatherless boy claiming a consul as father—these are typical of the inconsequential extensions with which legend thins out fact. But the facts are there to be recovered.

It should be noted that the boy prophesies that the red dragon of Britain, after three unsuccessful attempts would drive the English over the sea. By the end of the sixth century, and certainly by the beginning of the seventh, the white dragon of the English was firmly established in the island, and no prophecy of their expulsion could then have been written. The inclusion of this prophecy suggests that the story was first created when the Britons still hoped for final victory, and that the origins of the tradition are contemporary with Vortigern and the events described. Given this, the story of Nennius is not hard to decipher.

Vortigern, after deliberating with his council, travelled to the

West of the island to build or to renovate the defences. He met Ambrosius, still a young man, who warned him that his policy of settling the Saxons as Treaty Troops would prove fatal to Britain and who argued that the only solution was their expulsion from the island. Vortigern could not accept this, for it would have meant immediate and deadly war with the Saxons. Ambrosius emphasised that he was not only a prince of one of the States of Britain, but that his father held consular rank in the old Romanised government; Vortigern was not to place troops in his territory, nor to build defences there. The result was a watchful neutrality between the two leaders and Ambrosius, wedded to the idea of reviving the Roman systems of government, was content to let Vortigern return to his own territory and to his problems. Ambrosius may have known that his own time would come; and he was more likely to rally the States of Britain if he could show that he had taken no part in helping the disastrous policy of Vortigern. Vortigern would serve him better as a terrible example to set before his people than as a desperate and unpromising ally. For Ambrosius the title of Prince was nothing. It was pride in his Roman name, the memory of the consular rank of his father and the bitter conviction that the coming of the Saxons spelled the final doom of Roman Britain, which were the springs of his action and which legend records.

According to Gildas, the English now openly threatened that if their pay and supplies were stopped they would break their treaty and make war against the Britons. Their threats became deeds and according to the *Anglo-Saxon Chronicle* in 455 Hengist and Horsa fought with Vortigern the king at 'the place that is called Aylesford.' Horsa was killed in the engagement. The leader of the Britons is said to have been Vortimer, one of the sons of Vortigern. Aylesford is a crossing on the river Medway.

The Treaty Troops were attempting to fulfil their threat to ravage the whole island. Their first step had to be to effect the passage of the Medway. Eastern Kent is a mere promontory with the open sea to the east and south, and with the wide and sea-like estuary of the Thames to the north; from it, the river Medway is the only doorway to Britain. But Vortigern held the door firmly. The *Anglo-Saxon Chronicle* makes no claim for a victory at Aylesford, and Nennius, on the other side, says that the Saxons were driven back into Thanet. However it was a major and bloody revolt; according to one writer, the place became known in the British tongue as *Saessenaeg Habail*, the Slaughter of the Saxons.

Thus after eight years, Vortigern's policy had failed. At first successful allies, later sullen and discontented settlers, the Treaty Troops were now in open conflict with the army of Britain. The misgivings of Ambrosius had been vindicated. There were to be no more Treaty Troops. From now on the success of Britain depended upon the resolution and fighting quality of the army of Britain which, as Germanus had demonstrated, needed only a leader to achieve success. Two leaders in fact emerged: Ambrosius himself, and his successor Arthur.

On Vortimer's death shortly after the battle of Aylesford, the British resistance seems to have weakened, for the *Anglo-Saxon Chronicle* tells us that two years later, in 457, the Saxons inflicted a crushing defeat on the Britons at Crayford, where they claimed to have killed 4,000 men. The Britons, says the *Chronicle*, fled to London. With the whole of Kent in their hands and the Medway safely crossed, the Thames was the next barrier which the Saxons had to pass. But with London, which had impregnable defences, still in British hands, their advance paused. Concerning the next eight years the *Anglo-Saxon Chronicle* is silent, and presumably no further advances were made. A battle is mentioned for the year 465 in which twelve British leaders are said to have been killed. But as the *Chronicle* says that this was fought at a place called Wippedfleet, and that a Saxon officer called Wipped was killed there, the story may be a later invention inserted to explain the place name.

Some time before 473, the English (if we are to believe Nennius) fatally weakened the strength of British resistance by an act of terrible treachery. After Prince Vortimer's death, runs the story, Hengist offered peace and perpetual friendship to Vortigern. Vortigern's council decided that Hengist's proposals should be accepted. It was agreed that a delegation from either side should meet without arms to seal the new friendship. But before the meeting Hengist ordered each of his men to carry a hidden knife. (These curved knives were the characteristic weapons of the Saxons. Some believed that they took their name from these weapons, known in their language as *seaxe*; they are still the emblems of the counties of Essex and Middlesex.) The two parties sat down in friendship, each Saxon with a Briton beside him. Hengist called out his prearranged signal 'Saxons, take your seaxes!' and each Saxon knifed his neighbour. There perished 300 of the counsellors and officers of Vortigern. The Saxons did not kill the king but captured and fettered him, releasing him only after he had promised to grant them more territories, west of Kent for the South Saxons, and north of Thames for the East Saxons and Middle Saxons.

This story is given by Geoffrey of Monmouth with some additions. According to him the British dead amounted to 460— though they sold their lives dearly, fighting back with improvised weapons. Vortigern, he agrees, was captured and compelled to yield fresh territories in return for his release. After Vortigern was freed, says Geoffrey, the Saxons marched first to London which they captured and thence to York, Lincoln and Winchester. His geography is far less credible than that of Nennius!

Doubt must be cast upon the story of the knives since Gildas makes no mention of it: the treachery and the bloody murder at a friendly feast would have fitted so perfectly into Gildas's opinion of Saxon behaviour, that he could not have failed to use it had he known of it. On the other hand George Borrow, writing in the nineteenth century, asserts that the Welsh still remembered the event, referring to it as *bradwriaeth y cyllyll hirion*, the treachery of the long knives.

Finally in 473 came the final flare of war between the Saxons and the Britons. The *Anglo-Saxon Chronicle* has a laconic and terrible entry: 'This year Hengist and Esc (his son) fought with the Britons and took immense booty. And the Britons fled from the English like fire.' The reference to immense booty must mean either that the Saxons so completely broke the army of Britain as to have captured a great haul of their arms and armour, or that they took some great city. Gildas is speaking of the same event when, in describing the final rising of the English against the authorities of Britain, he writes: 'For now was kindled, caused justly by our earlier crimes, the eastern fire, fed by the hands of the heathen, from sea to sea.' The same image of the fire is used by writers on either side.

The army of Vortigern was swept aside or destroyed and the English roamed over wide areas of the island at will, swift as fire. And swift as fire was the retreat of the vanquished Britons. This was the final breakout of the English from their bridge-head in Kent; it was no longer revolt but conquest. Hengist, leader of a small number of Treaty Troops, had in twenty-six years grown to the stature of a potential Lord of Britain, a challenger for the ownership of the whole island. The fate that had overcome so many of the provinces of the Empire, of becoming kingdoms under barbarian kings, now faced the Roman Island.

In the perspective of history, it is easy to forget how wide a span is covered by a single human life. The Saxons had been in Britain over a quarter of a century, but Hengist still led them; he was to live to fight for another fifteen years; his career as leader of the English in Britain lasted forty-one years altogether. We must assume therefore that he was in his twenties when he brought his followers to Thanet. Thus he would have been born in 420 or thereabouts, some ten years after the fall of Rome and the death of Constantine III, and he lived to see the first beginnings of the country of England. In 473, a seasoned captain in his fifties, with long experience in governing his people in peace and war, he had openly made his bid for the ownership of Britain.

But there was another contender, one who had stood aloof and watched the fatal development of Vortigern's policy, but who was to stand aloof no longer—Ambrosius.

VII

AMBROSIUS—AND ARTHUR

IN Ambrosius's kingdom in the South West, Roman manners and methods survived. Without openly disputing Vortigern's claim to be Lord of Britain, Ambrosius kept his land apart and his army in being. This army would have been no local band improvised to defend a stretch of farmland, but a professional organisation, divided into cohorts with auxiliary cavalry and officered by tribunes and prefects. Roman weapons and discipline, as well as the Roman memory, were kept bright and ready, sustained by their leader's faith that their turn must come.

In 473, when the English broke out of Kent, and Vortigern's policy was finally discredited, the States of Britain knew that without a fresh leader and a new policy they would be overwhelmed by the barbarians, and that the patient building of 400 years would be shattered. Kings, consuls and tribunes; cities, states and villas; councils, governments and church—all would be swept aside by the jubilant Saxons, who had already shown what ruthless and destructive fighters they could be. As it was, the breakout of the English had terrible results. Gildas ascribed to it much of the ruin which in his day could be seen in the Roman cities of Britain. Even allowing for his usual exaggeration and for his lurid rhetorical descriptions, 473 was obviously an appalling year for the Britons. Many died in battle, many starved, large numbers took refuge in the hills and woods, whilst others crossed over as refugees into Gaul.

Minds turned to the patient Ambrosius, whose orderly kingdom showed the achievements of a ruler who thought more of
maintaining the old firm standards than of personal state. To it
and to his armies flocked the Britons from the ravaged territories;
in Gildas's vivid phrase, they came to him as eagerly as bees to a
hive when a storm is imminent. The separate detachments of the
army of Britain, with horses, arms and supplies, streamed along
the good Roman roads, to put their trust in their new saviour.
Ambrosius, too, identified himself and the cause of Britain with
the Christian cause in a way that Vortigern, who had used heathen
troops, could not. The people rallied to him, says Gildas,
strengthened by God and burdening heaven with uncounted
prayers.

What manner of man was Ambrosius, who had waited so long,
and who saw the coming of his hour of triumph and the renewal
of his hopes for the old ways of Roman Britain? Gildas says that
his full name was Ambrosius Aurelianus and that he was (doubtless in contrast to Vortigern) a modest man. He adds that he was
a Roman, the only one of his family who in the confusion of this
troubled time remained alive. In the legend of his meeting with
Vortigern he is shown as still a boy after the coming of the
Saxons; this probably indicates that even as a very young man
he had influenced affairs. He can be assumed to have been about
twenty years old in 447, when the Saxons settled in Thanet; as
his date of birth would then be about 427, Geoffrey of Monmouth's statement that he was a son of Constantine III, who
died some twenty years earlier, must be rejected. Moreover,
Procopius specifically states that the sons of Constantine had
been slain. But Geoffrey's claim could indicate that Ambrosius
was a kinsman of Constantine; a family link with an earlier
Emperor was often the basis of a claim to power, and Gildas
alleges that his parents had both worn the purple. Possibly the
descent was through his mother, for it is Ambrosius himself and
not his father the consul who was seen as the hope of Roman
Britain, and as Rome revived.

Now, in 473, Ambrosius was in his late forties; his reputation
as patriot and administrator, strong, patient and faithful, was well
established, but he was untried as a commander in the field. His
highly organised army, too, was—apart from the survivors of
units that had been defeated by the Saxons—untried in battle.
The Britons, wrote Gildas, now fought the war with Ambrosius
as their *dux*. This same Roman description was also applied to
Vortigern but, used of one as firmly Romanised as Ambrosius,
it undoubtedly has a deeper significance. Certainly, Gildas does
not call him king, as he does Vortigern. Nennius calls him *Rex
inter omnos reges*, king among all the kings of the British people,

STONE OF SECOND AUGUSTAN LEGION FROM HADRIAN'S WALL

implying that he was leader of all the regional kings. The stress
laid on his Roman background, the claim that his father was of
consular rank, the swarming to him of all the scattered army
of Britain, the statement that he had acted as *dux*—all these
hints justify the speculation that he formally revived the old title
of Duke of Britain. Had Vortigern done so, as he may have done,
it would have been mere vain-glory. If Ambrosius did so, it was
in a conscious attempt to revive the old forms, and to place his
loyalty to the concept of the Roman system above his loyalties
to the newer concept of tribal kings.

Against him stood Hengist the Saxon. Perhaps a few years
older, he too was a proved administrator, but he was also a
fighting commander with the marks of many battles on his

sword and armour. He had led his people across the wide North
Sea to the strange land of Britain. He had safeguarded their
interest in difficult negotiation; he had made a treaty on their
behalf that had brought them grants of land, pay and armour
and the opportunity of active service. He had shown himself able
to plan not only tactically but strategically, and had organised
reinforcements from his own folk in Germany, and from the
neighbouring tribes of the Angles and the Jutes. By ability
in the field against the Picts he had proved to the Britons the
value of his men, and had secured for them lands wider than
the little island of Thanet. When the time came for war with the
Britons he had not failed. At the bloody battle of Aylesford,
where great numbers of his men were slain, Hengist had fought
back grimly and stubbornly. Although the Britons held the field
they too had suffered bitter losses, and Hengist had brought the
survivors of his troops home again to fight another day. Cunning
in council, tough and brave in battle, he was a dangerous enemy,
with a career of success and victory behind him that was in itself
worth much.

These were the opposing champions. Their armies fought with
contrasting methods and for different motives. The army of
Ambrosius was the old army of Britain, re-grouped and re-
organised. The men obeyed their officers because they had been
disciplined and taught to do so. Their land had been attacked
and they were fighting in defence of their families and homes.
Defeat meant the end of their world, the destruction of life and
livelihood, with slavery as the only alternative to death. Their
religion, their economy, and their daily bread depended upon
the outcome.

But, beyond the immediate everyday things which they
defended, they were fighting for an idea. They knew, from their
fathers and from the great buildings and roads which covered
the land, how great and prosperous had been the Roman Island.
They saw that Ambrosius aimed to restore decency, decorum
and order to the land. They were fighting for the restoration of

happy times—the slogan that appeared on Roman coins which still circulated. They had much to gain, and everything to lose. The disciplined lines of their cohorts, the formal signal of trumpet and bugle, the respect paid to the standards and ensigns of their legions, the prayers of their priests, the smartness of their arms— these were not merely instruments for war; they were the signs and symbols of the world they hoped to rebuild.

Far different was the army of Hengist. His troops did not march in cohorts or legions but men of the same family, coming from the same village, stood together in his battle line. Not the formal discipline of the parade ground, but the discipline of kinship and loyalty bound his men to their officers. There was a tradition among them that, if their leader should be killed in battle, it was a disgrace for his followers to return home. To kill their leaders therefore brought an enemy no ease, but only more stubborn fighting; against a body of men which is resolved to die, even stronger enemies tend to crack.

Moreover, the English fought this war through choice: they took pleasure in fighting and in the loot which followed a success-ful battle. Where a Roman leader harangued his men to war with promises of glory and a reminder of past successes, a Saxon leader promised riches and booty. Tacitus had noted of their ancestors in Germany that they considered it shameful to gain by sweat what they could win by blood. A Saxon leader was praised by his men as the giver of rings, the bestower of treasure. War to them was a sport, and a profitable one. They were moti-vated by no conscious desire to found a new country; this came by accident out of the war-play. Immediate booty, immediate territory and immediate adventure were their selfish and uncom-plicated aims.

It was Britain's good fortune that both these peoples were to fuse and to develop a character somewhere between the entire Roman and the total German. Ambrosius and his great successor Arthur ensured this by their victories.

If Vortigern's policy of introducing the Saxons as Treaty

Troops had proved as successful as similar policies in the past, he would have been hailed by his contemporaries and remembered by historians as a saviour of Britain and a man of wisdom. But because the outcome was calamitous, he has been portrayed by the British chroniclers as villain absolute. It is hinted that he called in the Saxons as a deliberate act of treachery and his marriage to a Saxon bride is shown to be based upon drunken and uncontrollable lust. Because the war that developed between the English and the Britons was a war between heathen and Christian, Vortigern became the embodiment of all unchristian sins, is charged with love of luxury, avarice, treachery and incest, and shown as being rebuked by Germanus the bishop.

Ambrosius needed to demonstrate clearly his disgust with Vortigern's policy and, by some open and dramatic act, to foster and use the outburst of patriotic anger which followed upon its failure. So, according to Geoffrey of Monmouth, his first campaign was not against the English but against Vortigern. The clash between the pro-Roman and independent parties was now to be settled by force of arms.

Vortigern himself was not a war leader; rather did his genius lie in the council chamber. He left military leadership to his sons. One, Catigern, had fallen in the fighting at Aylesford. Vortimer, named by Nennius as victor over the Saxons, was also dead. The only surviving son, Pascent, is not described as a soldier. His army in disarray after the break-out of the Saxons, and without the support of any able general, Vortigern took refuge in a fortified town, and there (according to Geoffrey of Monmouth) Ambrosius besieged him. Ambrosius recalled the crimes of Vortigern, how he had introduced the pagans who had laid waste a fruitful country, destroying churches and almost extinguishing Christianity throughout the island. Ambrosius's army used siege engines against the town walls, a reminder that he had equipped his men in the Roman manner, and that he was still fighting a classical type of war. But he was using Roman methods of attack against a Roman defence work and the walls stood firm. Finally he set fire to the town, and Vortigern perished in the flames. Nennius confirms that Vortigern died when his stronghold was burned. But according to him Vortigern had taken refuge from the rebukes of Bishop Germanus and his clergy, and 'on the third night at the third hour, fire fell suddenly from heaven, and totally burned the castle.' Ambrosius may well have been seen as the instrument of Heaven, first rebuking and then destroying Vortigern for his sins.

Ambrosius now became the recognised leader of Britain—whether as the dominant king or as a purely military leader, the Duke of Britain, is not clear. That his power was supreme is indicated by the statement of Nennius that he permitted Pascent, the surviving son of Vortigern, to reign in part of his father's old kingdom. The goal of unity was more important for him than revenge. By allowing Pascent the status of royalty, he offered him grounds for gratitude rather than resentment. His own position clear, he turned his arms against the English in the South East.

He was not uniformly successful. Gildas, who as a great admirer of Ambrosius no doubt made his account as favourable as the facts permitted, describes the loyalty he evoked but makes no claim of unbroken or overwhelming military success. Nevertheless, the *Anglo-Saxon Chronicle* indicates that he succeeded very largely in holding back the English; from 473 until 490—a period of seventeen years—the *Chronicle* claims for them only one inland victory: in the year 477 Aelle came over from Germany with his three sons, landed in Sussex, slew many Britons, and drove some into the Weald of Kent as fugitives. But this was a mere skirmish from the sea, involving no inland advance.

The people who had rallied to Ambrosius almost in despair ('that they might not be brought to utter destruction', says Gildas) must have been encouraged now to hope for final victory. But Ambrosius was to do more than merely hold back the Saxons. Hengist heard the news of the victories of Ambrosius with terror, and breaking off his advance westwards, moved to the North.

This story may merely be a reference to the early English settlements on the north-east coast, or may describe a positive movement to the North by Hengist and his men. It would have been
logical for the Saxons to have swung northwards from the
Thames. They may have hoped to renew contacts with their
former allies the Picts, whom they had fought only at the instance of the Britons. Once north of the Wash, moreover, Hengist
could hope for assistance from the sea; reinforcements from
Germany could land along the north-east coast. Geoffrey mentions all these factors.

Ambrosius followed swiftly with his army, including a body
of cavalry. Hengist was defeated and captured by one of the
survivors of the meeting where the councillors of Vortigern had
been murdered. (This story confirms that some of Vortigern's
former followers had been among those who had rallied to
Ambrosius.) Hengist was beheaded, but Ambrosius treated his
dead adversary with honour, burying him in the Saxon fashion,
under a mound of earth. In the *Anglo-Saxon Chronicle*, Hengist's
coming to Britain and his victories are fully recorded, but his
death is indicated merely by the entry for the year 488: 'This
year, Aesc succeeded to the kingdom; and was king of the men
of Kent twenty-four years.' Such an oblique reference to Hengist's
death suggests that Geoffrey's story is true. Assuming Hengist to
have been in his twenties at the time of the landings, he would
thus have been in his sixties when he died.

Two years later, in 490, the Saxons took their revenge. For
Aelle and his son Cissa, having landed in Sussex, captured the
Saxon fort of Pevensey. The *Chronicle* claims that they
slaughtered all the Britons who were there. But in this defeat,
as in his victories, a constant purpose can be seen running
through the actions of Ambrosius. The inland advance of the
English being checked and Hengist having been defeated, the
Britons had re-occupied or were continuing to defend Pevensey;
they were again relying upon Roman works and Roman methods,
though this time in vain. Perhaps the walled fort gave insuffici-

ent opportunities to the cavalry which Ambrosius had used so effectively against Hengist; success for the army of Britain depended upon fighting a war of manœuvre, rather than a war of position. According to the *Chronicle*, this was the last inland defeat which the Britons suffered, until 508, when the Saxons claimed to have killed a British king and 5,000 of his men at Charford.

It has been suggested that Ambrosius was killed in this battle, described in the *Anglo-Saxon Chronicle* under that year as when Cerdic, leader of the West Saxons, 'slew a British king whose name was Natanleod'. But the evidence is scant and if our earlier assumptions are correct, Ambrosius would then have been over eighty. It is difficult to accept such longevity.

The *Anglo-Saxon Chronicle* claims that in 495 two Saxon chiefs came to Britain, Cerdic the leader of the West Saxons and Cynric his son, who fought with and defeated the Britons on the day they landed. It is tempting to take this as the battle in which Ambrosius died, but, it is only safe to say that he was born in 427 or thereabouts and probably died in or before 495.

He had achieved his task. His safe kingdom had provided a refuge for the defeated Britons when the English broke out of Kent. For fifteen years or more he had imposed upon the States of Britain, with their mixed populations and their separate and conflicting ambitions, a unity of command and of purpose. His unifying authority was recognised even by Pascent, son of his defeated enemy King Vortigern. The army of Britain had been restored as a fighting force, employing Roman methods. The English, sixty years after their arrival and thirty years after their first swift and dangerous advance, were still confined to a corner of the island, and the Christian cause had been defended. Ambrosius had brought back strength and hope to the Roman Island. Yet it was not round his name but round that of his successor Arthur that the legends were to grow.

Nennius writes that the Saxons increased in strength and numbers and that after Hengist's death Arthur was fighting against them in those days, alongside the kings of the Britons. The exact date when Arthur took command cannot be established; but it must have been after 488 if the evidence of the *Anglo-Saxon Chronicle* and of Geoffrey of Monmouth is combined, as indicated, and if Ambrosius captured and executed Hengist in that year.

From the scanty information available, it is clear that Arthur's career was no more uniformly successful than was that of Ambrosius. Gildas says that from the time of Ambrosius sometimes the citizens of Britan were victorious, but sometimes it was the enemies who conquered. When Ambrosius died, he bequeathed a united Britain as a legacy, his powers as well as his tasks being inherited in orderly fashion by his successor. But before Arthur died Britain was again divided and civil war had broken out. Arthur himself fell not by a Saxon sword, but in a war between two contending parties of Britons. Where Ambrosius had succeeded Arthur had failed, and his failure brought him death. It was his failure to retain unity among the cosmopolitan population of Britain, and not his military defeat at the hands of the English, that brought about the country's final overthrow.

With these contrasts in mind, it is at first difficult to understand why Arthur rather than Ambrosius became the central figure of the British legend. Yet within this difficulty there possibly lie not only the answer to the question itself, but indications of many other truths.

Two points are to be noted in particular. The first is that Arthur was much more definitely associated with the Christian cause than was Ambrosius. The latter was described as modest, strong and faithful: these are the classic Roman qualities. It is as a survivor of classical Rome that we see him. But Arthur, Nennius claims, carried an image of the Virgin Mary as a badge. This theme is echoed in other places. The Christian legend of the Grail became attached to the name of Arthur. Where Ambrosius called upon the Britons in the name of their Roman past, reviving old disciplines and skills and evoking the grandeur and duties they had known, Arthur used their present devotion and beliefs as his rallying cry. He recognised that if Roman qualities were to survive in Europe, they had to be identified with the Christian cause; and that the barbarians had to be conquered not only because they were seizing the island from the citizens but quite simply because they were heathens. He was fighting not only for the land of Britain but for civilisation. His motives and his greatness could thus be recognised by Christian elements throughout Europe. The ages that succeeded were Christian, and the acts of Arthur the Christian champion acquired a significance and permanence that were denied to the more ancient virtues of Ambrosius.

Arthur, of course, made no less use of Roman skills. We know that Ambrosius had a cavalry arm : his horsemen were in battle against Hengist. But later legends imply that Arthur had no other troops than his mounted men. He and all his companions are knights, fighting their battles exclusively on horseback. Whilst not representing the entire truth, this shows the image of Arthur that grew up; of a hero leading his mounted men on strange adventures and gallant rescues. He had understood, as the more classically minded Ambrosius had not, that the later Roman arm of the cavalry was now required almost to the exclusion of the earlier instruments of legions, infantry cohorts and siege engines.

Finally, his very failure was food for legend. Tragedy makes a more lasting impression upon men's minds than triumph. If Roland had marched as victor from Roncevalles, if Agamemnon the tall king had not perished tragically on his return from Troy, if Napoleon had died comfortably in Paris as the paunchy founder of a long and successful dynasty, can we believe that their names would have still sounded with the sound of trumpets, or that their legends would have taken on a magical power? The victories of Ambrosius are forgotten, and must be rescued from the curt sentences of the chroniclers. The death of Arthur in civil war, with the land he fought for divided, and facing defeat at the hands of his kinsmen and allies whom he had earlier led victoriously against their foreign enemies—these are the sorrows that made his life remembered and his death the centrepiece of legend.

But from his accession to power sometime after 495, to his death some forty years later, there are four decades of struggles and triumphs. The witnesses must be examined in detail.

VIII

THE TWELVE BATTLES OF ARTHUR

THE earliest witness to mention Arthur is Nennius, in his *History of the Britons*. According to R. W. Chambers, it was written down not later than AD 800-830 and not before AD 680, that is to say not less than 160 and not more than 300 years after the time of Arthur. Certain passages seem to draw upon earlier sources. Its general tone is reliable and scholarly; it it entitled to be given all the weight of a work into which older traditions have been incorporated, which is close to the period it describes, and which has been written or edited by a sober and careful hand.

After describing the death of Vortigern, and after a digression on the activities of St Germanus, Nennius writes:

In that time the Saxons increased in numbers and their strength grew in Britain.

When Hengist was dead, Octha his son crossed from the left hand side of Britain into the kingdom of the Cantii, and from him descended the Kings of the Cantii.

Then Arthur fought against those people in those days with the Kings of the Britons, but he himself was the *Dux Bellorum* or General in these battles.

The first battle was on the mouth of the river which is called Glein. The second, and the third, and the fourth, and the fifth upon another river, which is called Dubglass, and is in the kingdom Linnus. The sixth battle was upon the river which is called Bassas.

The seventh was the battle in the wood of Celidon, that is Cat

Coit Celidon, (which is 'The Battle of the Wood of Celidon' in the old British tongue).

The eighth was the battle in the stronghold of Guinnion, in which Arthur carried upon his shoulders an image of the Blessed Mary, the Eternal Virgin. And the pagans were turned to flight on that day, and great was the slaughter brought upon them through the virtue of our Lord, Jesus Christ, and through the virtue of the Blessed Virgin Mary, His Mother.

The ninth battle was fought in the City of the Legion. He fought the tenth battle on the shore of the river which is called Tribruit. The eleventh battle was waged in the mountain which is called Agned.

The twelfth battle was on Mount Badon where in one day nine hundred and sixty men fell in one charge of Arthur's. And no one laid them low but himself alone.

And in all these battles he stood out as victor.

The names given of the places where Arthur's battles were fought cannot now be certainly identified. This very difficulty argues the age and reliability of the passage, suggesting that Nennius was using old material in which British place names, now submerged under the new names given by the English, had been used. He does not attempt to make them comprehensible, but is content to repeat the older information. This is very different from Malory, Geoffrey of Monmouth and others, who write of Arthur's adventures in Winchester, Canterbury and other places whose names, in those English forms, did not exist in Arthur's day. Moreover, in the case of the seventh battle, after giving the Latin form *in silva celidonis*, he adds *id est cat coit Celidon*, giving the old British phrase for 'The Battle of the Wood of Celidon'. This supports the view that he is drawing from an older sources in which a language contemporary with the events was being used.

Nennius's report that after the death of Hengist his son and successor withdrew into Kent hints at a retreat by the English after Hengist's death which again suggests that his death was associated with a military reverse—supporting the story of his defeat and death at the hand of Ambrosius.

Next, Nennius makes it clear that Arthur was not himself a king. He fought together with the kings of the various States of Britain but (and the word 'but' adds emphasis to the distinction) he himself had the designation *Dux Bellorum*, or leader of the battles. Arthur's method of organising the British resistance to the invaders is now clear : he was continuing the revival of the Roman system begun by Ambrosius. Nennius could mean that Arthur consciously revived the title of Duke of Britain, or used some adaptation of it. It has been suggested that the title he revived was that of Count of Britain; but the counts were commanders of mobile expeditionary forces sent to the provinces by the central government. Arthur knew that any hope of a force from the Continent was now remote and that his sole hope lay in the army in Britain. The Duke of Britain had always been supreme commander of the garrisons and army groups in the island and the title would have been a reminder of past successes and a symbol that unity had been achieved, that the old military skills were again to be used, and that a well-organised and ably-commanded force was available. There is no need to reject or modify Nennius's words. Arthur, Duke of Britain, reviver of Roman forms and unifier of Britain, is a credible figure.

Nennius next lists the twelve battles which Arthur fought against the English. The first six are fought upon rivers, and no fewer than four upon a single river. These seem to be defensive rather than aggressive engagements. Presumably Arthur was trying to prevent the English from crossing into new territory, and the struggles for the crossings were renewed more than once. Although Arthur, according to Nennius, won all his battles, it is clear that at this stage he inflicted no defeat on his enemies sufficiently overwhelming to prevent them from making fresh attempts. We are reminded of the bitterly contested battle of Aylesford, forty or fifty years before, when the English had tried to cross their first river barrier, the Medway.

No one now knows where these battles took place. The British names which Nennius used have vanished. For the first, the battle of the River Glein, there have been many conjectures: there is a river Glen in Lincolnshire; there is a river Glen in Northumberland; and the Lun in Westmorland and the Leven in Cumberland have also been suggested. But we should look in the area where both strategically and tactically a battle was most likely to have taken place. Geoffrey Ashe *(Caesar to Arthur)* suggests that the Glen should be taken as being near the Wash, and there is much to support this.

As already seen the English made at least one sortie to the North, and one of the main tasks of the army of Britain would have been to prevent the English in the South East from joining forces with their hereditary northern allies, the Picts. If the first phase of Arthur's campaigns was aimed at pinning down the English within the south-eastern corner of the island, preventing any further movement north, then his first major battles would have been on the northern boundary of the area occupied by the English, somewhere along their line of communication with the Picts. This line was the Roman road from London to York, and it is somewhere along its southern stretch, at a point where it might easily be defended, that the first battle might have taken place.

From London the road ran slightly east of north, following the line of the river Lee. Thence, with only minor changes of direction, it ran to the important city of Lindum Colonia, the modern Lincoln, a walled city of great military importance. Forty miles south of Lincoln is the modern town of Bourne. Hereabouts, because of the great bay of the Wash, the road is only some twenty miles from the coast. To attempt to hold the road south of this point would be difficult. An enemy approaching from the south would have the width of Norfolk for manœuvre, and could easily work his way behind the defender's left flank. But at Bourne, the sweeping coastline approached the road. The Britons' left flank would have rested secure on the marshlands, and an enemy could make only a frontal attack.

Moreover about ten miles north of Bourne rises a small river, the Glen; it runs parallel with the road and to the west of it. As

it turns eastward to the Wash, the road crosses it. Here, strategically and tactically, is a place where a battle might well have
been fought—on a river Glen. Somewhere here perhaps, with his
right flank protected by the river and his left flank resting on
the marshlands, Arthur fought his first major independent engagement. If this was the northern frontier of the English and if
Arthur succeeded at this battle in establishing the Wash as the
northernmost point of the Anglo-Saxon advance, the county
name of Norfolk becomes significant. Here, for some years, lived
the most northern folk of the English. Though later they took
all the land up to the Wall, they were held here long enough to
give to this area the name (whose meaning is now lost in the
map of modern England) of the home of the North Folk.

To picture Arthur at this Battle of the River Glen we may turn
to the portraits of other men of this period on the later Roman
coins. We see him, probably still a young man, wearing an orna-
mented and embossed cuirass, and a close-fitting helmet with
protecting cheekpieces. He carries a slender horseman's spear and
probably a round shield. Remembering the traditions and successes of the past, he had reformed the cavalry units whose effec-
tiveness against the barbarians had so often been proved. Each
troop was led by an officer whose essential qualities had to be
both military skill and loyalty to the commander. These officers
were not merely his subordinates but his companions, as in former
days the counts had been the companions of the Emperors.

Perhaps at this battle there was a final charge down the wide
paved road when the heavy armoured horsemen moved with
levelled lances towards the bridge. The compact body of horsemen would gather speed until not even the obstinate bravery
of the English could stand against them, though many riders
would fall against the stubborn line of barbarians standing grimly
behind their shield wall. For the English, there was no retreat. To
retreat and flee was to be ridden down; to stand was at least to
have the chance, in the grim war play, of killing before being
killed.

After the charge, and after the trumpets had recalled the more impetuous horsemen from the chase, swords would be wiped and lances held at rest in hands weary from the fight. Amid the bitter smell of horse and leather and the sweetish smell of new blood, the men would gather the scattered arms and strip the dead of their armour. Swords, shields and helmets were of inestimable worth, and their harvesting was one of the fruits of victory. Later, over the silent field the ravens would gather and the wolves intrude.

The bridge was cleared and the leaders gathered to discuss the battle, and the points where it had gone well or ill. For the prisoners there was slavery; for the dead, the callous unarming and swift burial; for the defeated, the weary march south, and the resolution of revenge; and for Arthur and his companions, excited talk late into the night; the planning of the next move, the projecting of new units, and the everlasting hope of ultimate victory.

A northern frontier having been imposed upon the English, it was now necessary to check them in the West. By now the English had doubtless spread westwards from Kent, particularly along the southern coast, where in 490 the Roman fort at Pevensey had been taken. If the Romanised West, within which further armies could be raised and trained for the final victory, was to be preserved, the enemy's left flank had now to be engaged, and the English had to be held as firmly there as they had been to the north. This must have been Arthur's next preoccupation. After the victory at the River Glen, he would have left there one or more of his companions, with an army strong enough to stop any renewed attack up the road to York. But he himself, with the main body, turned southward.

The river Dublass of Nennius has been variously identified, for example as the river Duglas in Leicestershire. It is sensible however to seek a river whose modern name is a translation of the old British one. *Du* or *dhu* meant 'black' in the British tongue, and there are several rivers called Blackwater. One such is in

Hampshire, forming part of the boundary with Sussex. Here Arthur's strategy might well have brought him and this might well be the Dubglass of the battle.

The road from London to the West crossed the Thames at Staines, and thence ran to Calleva Atrebatum, near Reading. South-west of Ascot the old road, now known as the Nine Mile Drive and further west as the Devil's Highway, still runs straight and true between stretches of dark forest. South, and at right angles, flows the river Blackwater. With Calleva Atrebatum (Silchester) as his base, and with the Icknield Way as a link with his forces north-east of the Saxons, this would have been a logical place for Arthur to have begun his holding action to the west of the English. The river Blackwater (still a county boundary) would have provided a natural frontier behind which the English might be contained. Behind him lay Chichester on the coast, and inland the walled cities of Calleva Atrebatum and Venta (Winchester). These were now the heartland of Roman Britain, to be defended at all costs.

On Blackwater he met a more resolute enemy than had confronted him at Bourne. No one battle, no single charge of his horsemen, could achieve victory. For on this river were fought no fewer than four important battles. The intervals at which these were fought are unknown; the word Nennius uses is *bellum*, which means a war as well as a battle. So each may have been the climax of a campaign and the four wars on the river Dubglass may have covered a span of four years or more, with the English doggedly renewing their attacks each summer, and with Arthur as doggedly defeating them.

Although Nennius tells us that Arthur emerged victorious from all his battles, obviously here he had a hard-fought struggle, with final victory long in doubt. At this time there was in fact an opponent in the area who could have had the strength and persistence. This was Cerdic, leader of the West Saxons, who had landed in the island in 495.

The next battle is also on a river, the Bassas, the identification

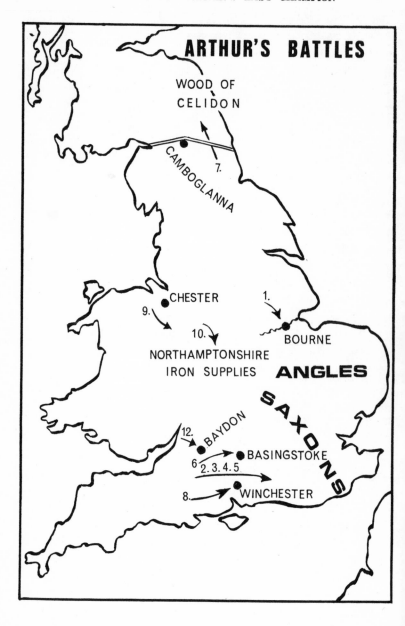

ARTHUR'S BATTLES

WOOD OF
CELIDON

CAMBOGLANNA

7.

CHESTER

1.

9.

BOURNE

10.

NORTHAMPTONSHIRE
IRON SUPPLIES   ANGLES

SAXONS

12. BAYDON

BASINGSTOKE

6 2. 3. 4. 5

8.

WINCHESTER

of which is lost. The suggestion that Basingstoke marks the site is feasible; it presupposes that after the engagements on the Dubglass, Arthur had withdrawn some few miles to the north-west. The name Basingstoke, considered to be of Saxon origin, not British, means the village built by the followers of a Saxon leader named Basa. But this leader may have given his name to a local river and the new name may have been current in Nennius's day. Geographically this site is not impossible, for here was Cerdic's country, the infant kingdom of the West Saxons.

The site of the seventh battle, the wood of Celidon, was probably north of the Wall, for the wood of Celidon is the wood of Caledonia. Since the English had not penetrated into these northern regions, Arthur was apparently faced by two entirely separate groups of opponents. To the south-east lay the English and their allies whom, by his successful campaigns, he had held firmly within a limited area. But in the North were the hereditary enemies of Roman Britain, the Picts. Although Arthur's successful battle on the river Glen had prevented the English from joining hands with the Picts, the latter were no doubt conscious of their opportunity. We know from the end of Arthur's story (for he was to die on the Wall in a civil war) that some northern Britons themselves were hostile to him, and the Picts may have found unexpected allies among these. So Arthur was forced to march northwards to put down a rising in southern Scotland. Again the stubborn line of the enemy, this time a mixed force of Picts and dissident Britons, would have received charge after charge of Arthur's heavy cavalry; again the victorious horsemen rode with poised spears at the broken enemy, overrunning their positions and destroying the last desperate resistance with downward thrusts of their bloody lances.

The eighth battle, at the Castle of Guinnion, might have taken place at Winchester, which in the Breton poem of Chrétien de Troyes is spelt 'Guincestre', or even at Windsor, which in the same text is spelt 'Guinesores'. Neither is geographically impossible, one being at the southern, the other at the northern extremity of Arthur's defensive line which held the Saxons from breaking out to the West.

It is likely that on his return from his northern wars, Arthur found the Saxons active in the South again, and that a campaign near the sites of his early battles became necessary. According to Nennius it was at this battle that Arthur bore the image of the Virgin Mary as his standard. The *Imaginifer*, a standard-bearer who carried the image of the Emperor, was a normal officer in the Roman army. Identifying the cause of Britain with the Christian cause, rather than with that of Imperial Rome, yet anxious to perpetuate the forms and practices of the past, Arthur substituted a Christian standard for the old Imperial ensign. But his particular choice is significant. With the Constantinian tradition so strong in Britain, and with Arthur's firm reliance upon the magic of things past, he might logically have revived Constantine's standard, the sacred monogram of Christ. He must have had very strong and positive motives for chosing another.

The Old Church at Glastonbury was dedicated to the Virgin Mary, and traditionally this dedication dated from apostolic times. If Arthur had been brought up in the Romanised western kingdom of Ambrosius, and if he had been a follower of the Marian cult of Glastonbury, his use of Mary's image as his standard becomes credible and reasonable. Nennius's statement points not only to the important part which Christianity played in the leadership and motives of Arthur, but also to the probability of a link between him and the Old Church of Glastonbury.

The ninth battle was at the 'City of the Legion', almost certainly Chester. This too was probably part of the campaign against the rebellious Britons of the North West. After the successful battle in the wood of Celidon, he might be expected to go on to reduce other points of resistance in the area. His own successes, which had lessened the dangers in the South East, were causing the urgent sense of a need for unity in the island to fade from men's minds. Not for the last time a man who had united a nation in the face of danger found that unity fading when his own effort began to defeat the external peril.

The tenth battle, the Battle of Tribruit, is documented in other sources than Nennius. The *Black Book of Carmarthen*, a medieval book of Welsh poetry, tells of one of Arthur's companions who came back with a broken shield from 'Tryvrwd'. To lose one's shield in battle had always been taken by the Romans as a sign of defeat and disgrace. (The poet Horace wryly admits to having left his behind at the battle of Philippi.) So this story conveys that

CATAPHRACT, FROM TRAJAN'S COLUMN

the victory was barely won, and that defeat had been narrowly avoided. The same poem tells us that the casualties were heavy : that one of Arthur's men killed his enemies three at a time, and another a hundred at a time. It also refers to 'the shores of Tryvwyd'. So Tribruit was a river and again this was a battle for a crossing. It cannot now be identified but it has been placed in the North, and may have been a resumption of the campaign that opened with the battle of Celidon. If so, then Arthur's opponents were again not the English but Picts and such of his own fellow countrymen as rejected his leadership.

The Britons in the North and North West could not see the

Saxon danger as vividly as those in the South : the independence of their own kingdoms was of more immediate importance than the safety of the island. They could see no urgent reason, divided as they were by long distances of hills and forests from the turbulent South East, for accepting Arthur as supreme commander of Britain. So the battle of Tribruit, like that of Celidon, may have been a battle fought by Arthur to establish his position as Duke of Britain. The kings in the North seemed content to recognise that the Saxons had come to stay permanently in the island. They saw Arthur as a greater danger to themselves and to their independence than the remote settlers south of the Wash and east of Winchester. On the shores of Tribruit, Arthur established his ascendancy, and made good his claim as military leader of the island. The *Black Book of Carmarthen* mentions one opponent by name, Eidyn, who may have been king of one of the northern states in Britain. The fact that this battle was fought between men of the same faith and country may account for its bitterness and the narrowness of the victory.

Malory is perhaps repeating the fact that Arthur was not accepted in the North but only south of the river Trent when he tells us 'that there should no man of war ride nor go in no country on this side Trent Water, but if he had a token from King Arthur.' In Malory's story one of Arthur's first battles is fought against a confederation of knights and kings from the North Country : 'Now shall we see,' says one of Arthur's allies with grim irony, 'how these northern Britons can bear the arms.'

Another possible reason for the battle of Tribruit emerges when the story of Excalibur is examined (Chapter XII). Arthur may have fought to defend the iron workings in Northamptonshire, near the modern steel town of Corby. With Continental supplies of arms no longer available, he would have reacted violently to any threat to his own iron industries. This too could explain the bitterness and fame of the battle.

The eleventh battle was fought on the hill called Agned. According to a marginal note in some of the manuscripts, this is in Somerset. If this is so, it would appear that while Arthur's main army was engaged in the North, the English had broken through in the South, and marched deep into the West Country.

This theory is borne out by the twelfth and most important of Arthur's battles, the battle of Mount Badon. Geoffrey Ashe places this at Badbury in Wiltshire, just south of Liddington. 'Badbury', as he points out, could be derived from 'Badon-Byrig', the fort of Badon. There is however another possibility. A few miles to the south-west is the small village of Baydon, standing on the old Roman road from Calleva Atrebatum northwards to Corinium, the modern Cirencester. North of the village rises the steep hill of Baydon, on the slopes of which can be still seen scars and ditches that may well be the vestiges of an old fortification. The first part of the name seems to be Saxon. The earliest recorded spelling of it (in AD 1146) is 'Beidona', and it is suggested that it was originally 'Beg-dun', the dun (or fort) where berries grow. But the Saxon word 'Beg' is merely deduced from the later spelling. On the other hand, the second half of the name is definitely British, revealing that there was a dun or fort here before the English came. So the mixed form of Beg-dun may never have existed, and the name may in fact indicate the Badon of Arthur's famous battle.

To the west, the ground falls steeply away. Here is the last high ground between the eastern part of the island and the plains of Wiltshire. Beyond it lay the rich city of Bath, and all the western States of Britain. We can imagine an English advance, while Arthur's army was in the North Country, over the disputed Blackwater and along the Nine Mile Drive and the Devil's Highway to Calleva Atrebatum. Without pausing to reduce that formidable city, with its virtually impregnable walls, the English host struck north-west, along the road to Newbury. Encouraged by news of growing disunity among the Britons, and knowing that Arthur's main forces were scattered between North and South and weakened by his struggles in the North, the English moved forward towards Corinium. They were not to be successful.

Indeed the *Anglo-Saxon Chronicle* reports that they did not seize the three prizes of the west, Gloucester, Cirencester and Bath, until 577—some sixty years later.

Gloucester was a legionary fortress and had been founded as a *colonia*. In this place, with its long military traditions, and with its barracks and store-rooms, no doubt part of the army of Britain lay. And perhaps it rode out along the straight road to Cirencester and beyond to meet the English host. Arthur fought alone this day, with his own personal army, and with none of the kings of the States of Britain. For Nennius says that the 960 casualties on the other side were caused by 'one charge of Arthur's. And no one laid them low but himself alone.' If the enemy had penetrated so deeply, Arthur's position was desperate, and all his earlier victories would have been meaningless had he been defeated so far to the west. He may have thought bitterly of the kings of Britain, who had failed to help at this crisis. During the days when the Saxons conquered, the States of Britain had been glad to follow him. But each king was now looking to his own kingdom. Some he had quelled by force; others held to him uneasily and suspiciously, jealous of their own local authority, and mindless of the island's total danger.

Perhaps, by penetrating so far to the West, the English were unwittingly helping his cause. Surely no British leader, whatever the outcome of this day's fighting, would ever again reject the need for a unified command. So might Arthur have mused, as he led his men up the long incline of the road, with the land falling steeply to his right, and the Saxon army somewhere in the high ground to his front.

The English it seems took refuge in the old hillside fortifications, for this battle has also been described by Gildas as a siege. To assault a hill fort is no task for cavalry. The steep slopes would slow down the charge, and the old ramparts stood between the attackers and their quarry. Arthur settled down to invest the fort in proper form. Deploying his men round the foot of the hill, out of bowshot but close enough to form an unbroken ring, he waited for thirst or hunger, or the exasperation that comes to fighting men cooped up defensively, to incite the Saxons to leave the safety of the fort. The siege lasted for three days. Then the English came out, to fight on open ground. At last Arthur's horsemen had room to charge; the slaughter of the Saxons was immense and Arthur's victory complete. The threat to the West was ended and no Saxon army ever fought a pitched battle against Arthur again.

The States of Britain for some years remembered the lesson of Badon, that the English peril was a continuing one and that in spite of Arthur's early victories there was always the danger of a sudden and unexpected thrust by the Saxons. The network of roads, an asset when the island was fully garrisoned, had now become a liability, giving opportunities of sudden mobility to the enemy. The need for a Duke of Britain, to watch over the whole island and to ensure the safety of what was left of the province, was clear. It was a paramount need that surpassed the local ambition of kings and regions. So for many years, while men remembered, there was peace and the victory of Badon appeared to be final.

IX

THE SECOND WITNESS

GILDAS the monk, according to the *Annales Cambriae*, died in AD 570. His book *De Excidio Britanniae* was written some time before 547, for this is the date of the death of Maglocunnus, one of the kings of Britain whom Gildas mentions as being still alive. Gildas was therefore writing at the latest ten years after the death of Arthur which took place, as we shall see, in 537.

Thus he was describing contemporary events when he wrote :

The Dux was Ambrosius Aurelianus, a modest man who alone among his Roman family (a faithful, strong and truthful count) had by chance survived amid this mighty storm, in which same storm his parents perished, who had both worn the purple. Whose stock now in our own time, sadly degenerated from its ancestral virtue, takes on strength, challenging the conquerors to battle, and to whom with God's help victory has been given.

From this time, now our citizens and now the enemy were victorious, so that in these people the Lord might test, in his accustomed manner, these new Israelites, whether they loved him or no; until the year of the siege of Mount Badonicus when was almost the last but not the smallest slaughter of these gallows-slaves and which was the forty-fourth year, as well I know, that arose, with one month already passed, which already is also the year of my birth.

But even now the States of our country are not inhabited as they were before. But to this day they are squalid, deserted and wretched, our wars with external enemies having ended, but not our civil wars. For both the terrible destruction of our island, and its unhoped for recovery, remained for a long time in those men's memory who were witnesses of both miraculous events. And because of this, kings, public officers and private men, as well as priests and churchmen all held the lines firm. But these having died and when a generation succeeded which was ignorant of that storm, and which know only the serenity and justice of the present, then the qualities of truth and justice were together broken and subverted so that of these qualities I would say not a vestige nor indeed any monument appeared in the above-mentioned classes of people, except among a few, and a very few indeed who, because of such a large number who daily run on all fours into hell, are held so small a number that venerable Mother Church does not see them who, her only true sons, recline in her bosom.

The style is confused, but Mount Badonicus is clearly the Mount Badon of Nennius. Gildas is telling us in a highly emotional manner of the recovery of the Britons under Arthur's leadership, and of the tremendous and final victory. His language as always is so charged with anger, bitterness and sorrow that it is hard to follow. But certain facts are clear.

After the death of Ambrosius there was a long struggle in which victory went sometimes to the Britons and sometimes to the English : this seems a more realistic account than that of Nennius with Arthur victorious each time. It helps to explain the four battles on the one river, and gives a further dimension to Nennius's flat tale. The battles were evenly fought with Arthur victorious, but not always decisively so, and they continued until the siege of Mount Badon, which was virtually the last and certainly the greatest slaughter of the English by the Britons. Arthur's long struggle here reached a successful conclusion, and until 547 the English never attacked again in any force. Nevertheless, although after Badon serenity and justice triumphed, the peace turned to civil war, as men forgot the terrible breakout of the English and the unhoped-for and abundant victory of Mount Badon.

After Badon, orderly life and government were resumed. The different classes of men, priest and layman, officer and private citizen, stood fast and performed their several functions. Civilisation came to flower again. But by the time Gildas was writing, all had changed. Civil war had broken out. The cities, which might have been rebuilt and re-organised, lay desolate and squalid. Hope and duty had both faded.

The disunity was not merely secular. Gildas tells us of his bitterness that Mother Church was failing to recognise her own true sons. Some few (among whom he no doubt included himself) were trying to maintain the old standards, but the Church was disregarding them. The centrifugal forces in Britain were now tearing apart the Church itself, the one institution which, in the absence of a military commander whom all would accept, might have brought back a political and spiritual unity to the island. That Gildas, devoted as he was to the Christian cause, could find it in his heart openly to criticise the Church is in itself evidence that the split went deep.

Three mysteries remain in Gildas's text. First, why does he not mention by name the victor of Badon, the man who wrought what he himself describes as a miracle? Second, what does he mean by telling us that the stock of Ambrosius, sadly degenerated from its ancestral virtues, was still alive in his day, achieving victory against the Saxons? Finally, what is he trying to say of of the date of Mount Badon, with his muddled reference to a period of forty-four years and to his own birth?

The reasons for Gildas's silence on the name of Arthur are intriguing. He is not prodigal with names. But he writes of Vortigern, whom he paints as a complete villain; he refers to Ambrosius in some detail, sketching in his virtues and his Roman descent. If he thought it worth while to mention Ambrosius, why did he not write of Arthur his successor, the victor of Badon and the man who brought back peace and justice to the island? There are two possibilities which, together, would explain this extraordinary gap in Gildas's story.

The first is that he and Arthur had been on different sides in the civil wars and in the ecclesiastical quarrels that ensued. If this were so then Gildas, emotional and easily moved to anger, would have been psychologically incapable of writing the panegyric on Arthur that the victories deserved; yet he might have been prevented by old loyalties, by a recognition of all that Badon had done for the island, from painting Arthur as a villain. Gildas was unable to write a balanced portrait: a man had to be all hero or all villain. Present anger conflicted with past gratitude and he could not paint Arthur as either. Gildas, who had no control over his own rhetoric which would gallop down long avenues of anger, took refuge in silence. Indeed, Giraldus Cambrensis records a tradition that Gildas had written of Arthur, but cast his book into the sea.

The second possibility is that Gildas did refer to Arthur in his book, but did so obliquely. Such references would have been clear enough to his contemporaries who would have been made aware of his opinions; while Gildas himself was saved from the charge of ingratitude, and freed from the temptation to inveigh openly against the hero of Badon.

For the first possibility, the quarrel between Gildas and Arthur, we have some evidence. There are two biographies of Gildas, one written in the ninth century and one compiled in the twelfth century at Llancarfan. According to the latter, Gildas was one of the many (twenty-four) sons of Nau, a king of the North. Nau is said to have been a king of the Picts. Gildas's origins thus seem to have been in an area where Arthur had enemies even during the height of his career. The biography goes on to tell us that Gildas was a contemporary of Arthur 'whom he diligently loved, and whom he always desired to obey'. However, his twenty-three brothers resisted Arthur. The eldest, Hueil (described as an assiduous warrior and most famous soldier) is said to have obeyed 'no king, not even Arthur', and was finally captured and slain by Arthur. Gildas wept at the news and mourned bitterly the loss of his dear brother. Daily he prayed for his brother's soul, where before he used to pray daily for Arthur, his brother's persecutor and murderer.

If this story contains a genuine tradition, it gives a credible explanation of the tense ambivalence of Gildas's feelings. Arthur had fought for the cause in which Gildas most fervently believed—the cause of Christianity against heathendom. He was a leader whom Gildas desired to follow and to obey. But, by the kind of chance which civil war makes all too common, his hero had become the executioner of his brother. To one as volatile and emotional as Gildas, the shock and horror must have been traumatic. Maybe the monk and patriot continued to support Arthur with his reason; but the brother grew to hate him with his heart. A more balanced pen than his would have been needed to describe the glory of Arthur's cause, the miracle of his victories, and the terrible intensity with which he pursued his purpose, killing the writer's own brother for defying his authority : and killing him not in fight, but executing him after capture when pardon might have been possible.

Politically, in fact, Arthur had no choice of action when Hueil fell into his hands during some civil struggle in the island. If the English were to be checked, he had to impose his authority over all the Britons and to re-establish internal peace and unity, at whatever cost. So Hueil was executed for a cause that Gildas supported, and for reasons that Gildas knew to be good but could never accept. The victor of Badon had the blood of Gildas's brother on his hands. The victory was great, but Gildas could not find it in his heart to celebrate the victor.

One of his oblique references to Arthur has long been recognised. After describing the final destruction of Britain in the civil wars that followed Badon, Gildas addresses a series of rebukes to the leaders of Britain, pointing out to them their sins. He asks King Cuneglass:

> Why have you fallen back into the sewage of your former wickedness? Indeed, from the years of your youth you, the Bear, have been the rider over many men, and the driver of the chariot which carried the Bear; you are a despiser of God, and an oppressor of his order, you Cuneglass whose name, in Latin, means 'The Yellow Butcher'.

The Celtic word for bear is *arth* or *artus*, and in describing Cuneglass as 'driver of the chariot which carried the Bear' Gildas may be reminding him that he once drove Arthur's chariot. The fact that in the same sentence Gildas translates the name Cuneglass into its Latin equivalent shows that his mind, at the moment of writing, was working bilingually, flowing between the British and the Latin tongues. Gildas's contemporaries would have been quick to recognise this play on words.

The second possible allusion seems hitherto to have gone unnoticed. This is the mention by Gildas of the progeny of Ambrosius. They are described as alive at the time of which Gildas is writing; as victorious with the help of God over their enemies the Saxons; and yet as having fallen sadly below the standards of virtue of their great ancestor. Here is the very kind of ambivalence to be expected in the light of the Hueil episode. Gildas cannot detract from the merit of Arthur's victories, nor from the fact that they were won in the Christian cause. Yet Arthur (if this indeed is a reference to him) is described in spite of his victories as falling short of the virtues of Ambrosius. What was the particular virtue in which he was lacking? Perhaps it was clemency, the magnanimity to forgive a captured enemy.

And what does Gildas mean by his reference to the descendants of Ambrosius? For a hint we must turn to the *British History* of Geoffrey of Monmouth. As already noted, Geoffrey claims to have based this on 'a very ancient book in the British tongue' given to him by Walter, Archdeacon of Oxford. As his work contains many wild and impossible statements it has been argued that the 'very ancient book' never existed, or that at any rate Geoffrey was not a simple translator but a spinner of fables. Nevertheless, his history may contain some traditions not preserved elsewhere. Where it can be taken as supporting other evidence, it must not be excluded from consideration.

Geoffrey alleges that on his death Ambrosius was succeeded by his brother Uther Pendragon, and that Arthur was the son of Pendragon, and therefore the nephew of Ambrosius. If this legend contains only an element of truth, it makes Arthur at any rate a kinsman of Ambrosius. Gildas's reference to the progeny of Ambrosius thus becomes explicable. Arthur was not only the successor but also the (possibly collateral) descendant of Ambrosius. The allusion would be readily understood by the contemporaries of Gildas. Arthur had certainly challenged the English conquerors to battle, and had with God's help gained the victory. Nevertheless in the eyes of Gildas he had fallen from the high standards of Ambrosius.

Perhaps the comparison with Ambrosius was an unfair one : Ambrosius had no problem but the defeat of the Saxons. A desperate and frightened Britain united behind him and recognised his authority. Arthur, with the panic fear of the Saxons stilled, had to face the reviving ambitions and independence of the States of Britain. The work of Ambrosius was in danger, and the whole concept of a single commander of the armies of Britain had been put in jeopardy by the revolt in the North. Through stern discipline Arthur had to demonstrate his power and as Duke of Britain to impose a new unity. After Celidon and Tribruit he could not afford mercy. So Hueil was executed, and Arthur's name was banished by Gildas and a slur cast on his memory.

The third problem set by Gildas is his reference to Mount Badon and to a period of forty years for its dating. The battle is also mentioned in the summary history known as the *Annales Cambriae* or *Annals of Wales*, the manuscript of which was transscribed in the eleventh or early twelfth century. This was copied from an earlier manuscript completed in the tenth century and contains brief entries for each year, the last entry being for 977. Some were compiled much earlier than this, for there are twenty blank years after 954, as though this was the final entry of a yet older manuscript which a later copyist had intended to continue.

Where the accuracy of some of the earlier information can be checked, the document appears to be reliable. For example, the entry for the year 613 mentions the battle of Cair Legion. A quite independent chronicle, the *Annals of Tigernach*, gives the same date for the same battle. Moreover, the *Annales Cambriae* tells of the death of Maglocannus (one of the kings of Britain) in 547 'of the great mortality.' We know from other sources that the plague was rife in Europe in 543-4, so that it would indeed have visited Britain in about 547.

The entry for the Battle of Badon is made under the year 516 and reads: 'The Battle of Badon in which Arthur carried the Cross of Our Lord Jesus Christ for three days and three nights on his shoulders and the Britons were victors.' So three days and nights was the time needed to goad the English, by thirst and by hunger, to their desperate and vain sally from the ramparts of the hill fort. Then we are shown Arthur carrying as his standard a Christian emblem—not that image of the Virgin Mary which Nennius tells us was borne at the Battle of Castle Guinnion, but the Cross of Christ. Again the struggle of the Britons is seen as a defence of Christian civilisation against the barbarians. Finally, a specific date for the Battle of Mount Badon emerges, 516. This must be checked against Gildas's confused reference to forty-four years. The late R. G. Collingwood, in his book *Roman Britain and the English Settlements,* made a careful analysis of the problem, which still leaves the date of Badon an open question.

Collingwood takes the statement of Gildas as meaning that the battle took place forty-four years before the time that he was writing, and that moreover it took place in the year when he was born. But we know that Gildas was writing some time before 547 (because in that year King Maglocunnus died, and Gildas writes of him as still alive). Therefore, Collingwood argues, the battle must have taken place at least forty-four years before that date, namely in 503 or earlier. This date conflicts sharply with the *Annales Cambriae,* and as Gildas was a contemporary of the events he describes, and since he mentions such a precise and cir- cumstantial period as forty-four years, his evidence is to be pre- ferred.

There is one other source of evidence. Bede, the English historian, writing about 200 years after Arthur's battle, was a critical and exact scholar, who made full and careful use of earlier material. From his chapters on these events, it is evident that he was using the works of Gildas, for he follows Gildas's text closely—in many parts word for word. In his account of the Battle of Badon he is clearly copying out whole sentences from Gildas. Yet in this particular passage he makes minor modifications and one significant change. Here are the two passages.

GILDAS	BEDE
And from this time, now our citizens and now the enemy were victorious (so that in these people the Lord might test, in his accustomed manner, these new Israelites, whether they loved him or no),	And from this time now our citizens and now the enemy were victorious
until the year of the siege of Mount Badonicus which was almost the last but not the smallest slaughter of these galows-slaves, and which was the forty-fourth year, as well I know, that arose, with one month already passed, which was also the year of my birth.	until the year of the siege of Mount Badonicus when they inflicted not the smallest slaughter upon their enemies in about the forty-fourth year from their coming into Britain

The important change made by Bede is that the period of forty-four years is now counted from the coming of the English into Britain. Bede was separated by only 200 years from the time of Gildas, and may have been in possession of an earlier copy of his works than we possess. Bede's paragraph, which has all the marks of a careful copy, may thus be (with minor modifications) what Gildas actually wrote. If so, then the text known today of the works of Gildas is corrupt, and it is some copyist's error, rather than the faulty style of Gildas himself, that makes this passage so hard to understand.

Pursuing this argument, if Gildas's date for the coming of the

English into Britain is fixed, and forty-four years added to it, a
true date for Badon is found. Bede gives more than one date for
the arrival of the Saxons into the island. If as Collingwood suggests we take 446, the date for Badon is 490, which again conflicts with the *Annales Cambriae* and brings no solution.

There is, however, another way of interpreting the evidence
which goes far to reconcile these facts. First, it can be accepted
that Bede's paragraph represents very closely what Gildas wrote.
Bede has merely omitted the reference to the coincidence that
the year of Badon was also the year of the birth of Gildas, which
personal aside was not to Bede's purpose and would have been out
of place in his work. Assuming Bede to be correct, the period
of forty-four years must be counted not backwards from the time
of writing, but forwards from the coming of the English 'into
Britain'. The present suggestion is that this coming of the English is not to be taken as their first settlement as Treaty Troops.
Indeed, on that occasion they could hardly be said to have come
'into Britain', being settled in and confined to the tiny Isle of
Thanet. The date of their first limited and legal settlement (446),
which Collingwood suggested as Bede's fixed point, is unlikely to
have been taken by Gildas and the Britons as the real date of the
entry of the barbarians into Britain proper.

Surely, they would have meant the year when the Saxons broke
out of the lands within which they had been settled and to which
they had legal title. This happened, as we have seen, in 473. This
was the terrible year when the English came into Britain like a
fire; the year in which Vortigern's policy was discredited; the year
in which Ambrosius raised his standard; and the year from which
no doubt the Britons dated their full-scale war against the invaders of their country who, until that date, had been not
invaders but allies.

If we add the forty-four years to this date we reach 517, which
agrees to within one year with the *Annales Cambriae* and which,
it is suggested, should be taken as the date of the Battle of Badon.
Then what Gildas was trying to tell us, through the confusion

of his own style and the errors of the copyists, would have been somewhat as follows:

> And from that time, now our citizens, now the enemy, were victorious (so that in these people the Lord might test, in his accustomed manner, these new Israelites, whether they loved him or no), until the year of the siege of Mount Badon, when our citizens inflicted almost the last and the greatest slaughter upon these gallows-slaves; which year was, as I know, the forty-fourth from their first coming into Britain; and which was also the year of my birth.

If we accept this date for Badon, certain further deductions can be made. Gildas was born in the same year, 517. The *Annales Cambriae* says that he died in 570: he would thus have been fifty-three years old when he died, which is entirely credible. We have already seen that he was writing before 547; he would have been just under thirty at that time. He thus wrote his book not more than thirty years after the Battle of Badon. This again is credible, for the period would have been long enough for a new generation of public officers, private men, priests and churchmen to have grown up, as Gildas tells us, ignorant of the great struggle with the English, and forgetful of the desperate need for civic virtues and unity.

This scheme of dating also means that Hueil was not executed during Arthur's main struggle against the English, for that had been completed at the Battle of Badon, before the birth of Gildas. Hueil's revolt against Arthur must have come towards the latter end of Arthur's life, during the period of disunity and civil war that culminated in his death at the hands of Mordred. Hueil's death becomes one link in the chain of events that led to the field of Camlann.

Arthur died, according to the *Annales Cambriae*, in 537, twenty years after the suggested date of the Battle of Badon. Some confirmation of this, at least of a negative kind, might be expected in the *Anglo-Saxon Chronicle*: there ought to be no claims of any substantial advances or victories by the Saxons from 517 until after 537. And we find just that kind of silence for this period. In 514 the *Chronicle* claims that in a battle at Cerdic's-ore, 'the Britons were put to flight'. But this phrase is not used again until 552. In the years between, we are simply told that the West Saxons 'fought with the Britons' at Cerdices leaga, and that is all. This negative evidence is significant if the Saxons had in fact suffered a crushing defeat in 517; skirmishes would subsequently take place and be reported but no engagement occurred which the chronicler, however partial, could possibly claim as a victory.

ANDERIDA (PEVENSEY)

Not until 530, when the Saxons claim to have taken the Isle of Wight, is there a report in the *Anglo-Saxon Chronicle* of further fighting. Perhaps by this time the civil war was beginning, with Arthur now facing revolt in the North. Cerdic, leader of the Saxons, may have taken the opportunity for a further seizure of land; but after the terrible lesson of Badon, and at a time when—according to Gildas—the officers of Britain were doing their duty (at least in the South), he dared not or could not strike westwards into Britain proper. The Isle of Wight lay to the south of the region within which he had been contained, and to take that was relatively easy.

Four years later Cerdic died, with no further advances to his credit. In 552, thirty-five years after Badon and fifteen years after the death of Arthur, the *Anglo-Saxon Chronicle* does speak again of the Britons being 'put to flight'. In this year the English took Salisbury, and the western lands lay open to them. But Arthur's victory at Badon had held back the tide for thirty-five vital years, during which the Britons and the English remained in sullen and suspicious contact, and during which the new character and form of the country was being moulded.

The length of time is a measure of the greatness of the victory. Had Arthur but found a successor, as Ambrosius had done, the history of England could have been mightily changed, and the history of Britain might have continued for centuries.

X

COMPANIONS AND ADVERSARIES

WHEN any officer, civil or military, was commissioned by the Roman government, he received a formal document of appointment. This listed the staff to which he was entitled or the military units that came under his command. It also showed the badge of his office. These badges were sometimes formalised maps of the territory where he was to serve, or pictorial symbols of the matters under his control.

The officer who issued these documents was the *primicerius notariorum,* or chief appointments secretary. Claudian, the fourth-century poet, has given us a description of this chief secretary's duties.

> He issues the documents of official appointments. He organises the garrisons of the provinces, holding in unity the Empire's widely distributed forces. Carefully he studies the positions of the different troops—what regiment keeps guard on the Sarmatian shores, what units stand against the fierce Getae, what legions hold back the Saxons and the Scots, how many cohorts encircle the shores of the seas, and how many troops maintain the peace on the Rhine river.

The chief secretary kept a record of all the offices in the Empire and this central register was known as the *Notitia Dignitatum.* Fortunately, transcripts of one of these lists, probably that for the year AD 428, have survived : the original has vanished, but four excellent copies made in the fifteenth and sixteenth centuries show in detail the network of offices throughout the Empire.

Because when Bishop Germanus came to Britain in 429 he found no Roman officers, we might expect this register of 428 to contain no reference to the island. Yet it contains a full list of the offices in Britain, as if Roman rule still persisted there. Probably the central government had not abandoned all hope of bringing Britain back into a restored Empire. The Note of Honorius was not a formal recognition of Britain's independence. On the contrary, it expressed the intended continuity of Rome's authority. The States of Britain would have battled on alone without Rome's instructions and by ordering them to do so Honorius made it appear that Britain was still obedient to his authority. The register of 428 shows, as it were, the shadow government of Britain, recording the conditions of rule which Rome hoped to revive.

The first to be listed are those who came under the direct command of the *vicarius* or governor general. These were the provincial governors of the five provinces into which the diocese of Britain was divided. Two, Maxima Caesariensis and Valentia, had provincial governors of consular rank; the remaining three had governors of lower status.

The register includes the office of the Count of Britain and defines his responsibilities. His badge was an island on which was drawn a single city with turrets and bastions, crowded with clustering buildings. There is also the Duke of Britain, who was in charge of the permanent military establishments and had a badge symbolising this: an island holding fourteen walled towns. The list of officers under his command shows the formidable array of the army in Britain—the army which Rome was still hoping to re-establish. First came the prefect of the Sixth Legion, then the prefects of the independent cavalry units; two of these units are described as horsemen, and the third as *cataphracti* or armoured knights. Then follow the commanders of various detachments: there were twelve in all, so that the three cavalry commanders accounted for a quarter of the roll. Next came the commanders along the line of Hadrian's Wall. Although by now the Wall was no longer manned, the troops which Rome had once used for its defence are listed. The names of the detachments show the wide area from which Rome enlisted her armies, and bring echoes of the many languages spoken in Britain: Dalmatians, Gauls, Tungrians and Spaniards are included. The names of their proud garrison towns are changed, and their walls have crumbled; their memorials are the formal drawings on the badge of the Duke of Britain (reproduced on page 8).

Then came the Count of the Saxon Shore, whose badge shows the forts that guarded the invasion coast. Among his officers are listed the prefect of the Second Imperial Legion and the commanders of two units of cavalry.

This document, or a copy of that part of it which referred to Britain, would have been available to Arthur and would have shown him the strength of the old Roman army in Britain, and the officers appointed there during Roman days. To any man of imagination in those times the names of the armies of the Duke of Britain and of the Count of the Saxon Shore were not only a memory, but a challenge. Was it possible, without help from Rome, to rebuild the garrisons, to refit the army, to remount the cavalry and to drive the barbarians into the sea? This was the dream that Arthur dreamed and which, for a magic while, he fulfilled.

In the register Arthur would have found four senior posts in Britain, any of which he could have considered as appropriate for him to assume himself. First was the *vicarius* or governor general of the diocese. Although he was the supreme officer of Britain, holding all that was left of the Roman authority, Arthur as a military leader would have decided that the title of the civil governor was not a suitable one for him. Later, as his organisation prospered, he may have appointed one of his men to this office. Next was the *Comes Brittaniarum* or Count of Britain, a proud and evocative title, recalling the great Theodosius and Stilicho, as well as all those men who had been Companions of the Emperor from the earliest days of the Empire. But this title had been given to men who came to aid a distressed or beleaguered province, leading an expeditionary force chosen from the armies of the Empire. Arthur had no such force at his command. Some few men may have come to the island from Armorica and Gaul to help him, but of formal reinforcement there was none. So the title would have been an empty one.

The other office to bear the title of count was that of Count of the Saxon Shore, who guarded the South East of the island from the Germanic invaders. By Arthur's time, with Kent firmly held by the English and with the whole of the South East overrun, this title would have been a nominal one; in any case it was of purely regional significance and this too Arthur must have rejected.

There was left the post of Duke of Britain, commander of the permanent garrisons of the island. This was the post which Arthur seems to have occupied, and is the title which would have fitted his position. If Arthur is placed in the pattern of the *Notitia Dignitatum*, then the Companions of Arthur, those who have come riding down to us in medieval disguise through the pages of legend as the knights of the Round Table, must be sought in the same pages among the subordinates or colleagues of the Duke of Britain.

In his Book III, Malory tells of the wedding of Arthur to Guener, daughter of King Leodagrance. As a wedding gift, King Leodagrance sends Arthur the Table Round, which he himself is said to have received from Uther Pendragon. With it he sends 100 knights, and Arthur bids Merlin, his counsellor, find fifty knights to make up the company. 'Within short time,' writes Malory, in Chapter II of this book,

Merlin had found such knights that should fulfil twenty and eight knights, but no more he could find. Then the Bishop of Canterbury was fetched, and he blessed the sieges with great royalty and devotion, and there set the eight and twenty knights in their sieges. And when this was done Merlin said, Fair Sirs, you must all arise and come to King Arthur for to do him homage; he will have the better will to maintain you. And so they arose and did their homage, and when they were gone Merlin found in every sieges letters of gold that told the knights' names that had sitten therein. But two sieges were void.

Does the *Notitia Dignitatum* give some lead to this figure of twenty-eight, and perhaps some clue to the two void sieges? Details are given, as already said, of the commands of the three principal officers, the *vicarius* or governor general, the Count of the Saxon Shore and the Duke of Britain. Under the *vicarius* came the governors of the five provinces into which Britain was subdivided. The Count of the Saxon Shore had nine garrison commanders, one for each of the forts along the shore. Under the Duke of Britain were fourteen commanders all bearing the title *praefectus*, including the commander of one legion (the VI), several commanders of cavalry, and commanders of various other detachments. There were also nominally twenty-three garrison commanders of forts along the Wall. But for many years these had remained unmanned, and it would have been unrealistic for Arthur to have planned to reoccupy them, or to have appointed officers to do so.

The Saxon forts were another matter. Should victory ever be as complete as Arthur dreamed and the English be driven from the island or brought under his domination, then the reoccupation of the forts in the South East would be a matter of urgency. It was not unreasonable to contemplate a time when Dover, Pevensey, Lympne, Richborough and the others would once more see the Eagles, and once more receive detachments of his troops. He may have appointed officers for these forts partly as a symbol of his optimism and intentions.

Thus the full strength of Arthur's shadow government and commanding officers would have been :

Vicarius, Count of the Saxon Shore and Duke of Britain	3
Under the *vicarius*, the provincial governors	5
Under the Count of the Saxon Shore, the commanders of the forts	9
Under the Duke of Britain, the garrison commanders and commanders of units (excluding those of the Wall) ...	14
Total	31

Since Arthur himself was Duke of Britain, we should expect to find a total of thirty companions. But two of the five provincial governors had to be of consular rank, appointed by the central government itself in Rome: Maxima Caesariensis and Valentia were provinces of especial importance, each named after an Emperor—Galerius Maximianus and Valentinus. Arthur was not a representative of the central government, but a local champion; he may have hesitated to appoint two officers who ought to have been of consular rank and nominees of Rome. In this way the total number of his officers would have been twenty-eight, and there would have been two vacancies to be filled at a later date. Thus Malory's figure of twenty-eight knights is consistent with the *Notitia Dignitatum*, as is his account of the two void sieges.

It seems that here, in the midst of an apparently fabulous tale, emerges an old and accurate tradition, and that the Round Table is the grand council of the Duke of Britain, the assembly of all Arthur's commanders and subordinates. After the tragedy of Camlann, men would have remembered the days when Arthur guided the destiny of the island through the strength of his subordinates and companions who came to be remembered as knights errant. Indeed this conception is not far from the truth; as commanders of cavalry detachments, they did in fact range widely over Britain, righting wrongs and challenging the might of the invading English. Something more than merely verbal tradition appears to have handed down the precise number of twenty-eight and the strange story of the empty chairs.

It is possible that after Arthur's death a chronicle of his life was written. In it would have been an account of how he achieved supreme command, together with the names of his chief sub-ordinates and adversaries, and the story of how in the end the armies of Britain became divided and there was civil war, ending tragically in the field of Camlann.

If such a chronicle ever existed, it was probably lost fairly early. Arthur's fame had largely to depend upon oral tradition, upon the inaccurate recounting from generation to generation of his achievements which became confused, as we have seen, with the story of Maximus. But the lost chronicle could have survived long enough to merge with the oral tradition, and to graft on to it some precise details, such as the number of the commanders holding office under Arthur, as well as some of their names. Caxton, who first printed Malory's book, tells us that Malory 'did take (it) out of certain books of French, and reduced it to English'. Moreover, while asserting that Arthur was a real figure and that those who thought otherwise were guilty of 'great folly and blindness', Caxton implies that there is a great deal of fiction in Malory's version. 'For to give faith and believe that all is true that is contained herein, ye be at your liberty.' Perhaps in the many books of which Caxton tells, in Dutch, Italian, Spanish, Greek, French and Welsh, some echoes remained, perhaps garbled and hard to recognise, of the lost Chronicle of Arthur. Traces may have survived in Malory's own compendious collection of the traditional tales; there appear to be other instances as well as the story of the twenty-eight knights. Immediately after the appointment of this first company, Arthur is said by Malory to have set his own nephew Gawaine in one of the two vacant places. (Gawaine, or Wawain as he is called in some of the stories, is well attested in many different texts.) This suggests that he was placed in charge of one of the two special consular provinces, some time after Arthur made his first appointments. Arthur had felt diffident at using the two consular posts, and it is possible that, when he finally came to fill one of them, he chose a member of his own family; since he himself was by now the embodiment of the Roman authority in the island, this was the nearest he could come to the appointment of a representative of the central government of Rome itself.

This still left vacant one place at the assembly of officers. Perhaps this was the Siege Perilous of the stories: a seat which none might occupy until the dream had been fulfilled of re-establishing contact with Rome, who would herself nominate the holder. Until that dream faded this post lay vacant, as a sign of Arthur's hope that Britain would once again become the Roman Island. It was also a symbol of his care to make no appointments that might lay him open to a charge of usurpation. But the dream faded, and it became clear that formal links with Rome were not to be forged. So the Siege Perilous was filled by Galahad. Galahad was the son of Launcelot, so this appointment must have come late in the history of the Companions. The hope of the Roman Island had lasted long enough for a second generation of officers to grow up, and this adds significance to Arthur's appointment of his own nephew to the first of the vacant places.

Assuming this part of Malory's narrative to contain traces of the real events let us look more closely at the figure of Launcelot. A significant fact is that he has two names. Malory calls him Launcelot, but says that his son Galahad was given this name 'by cause Sir Launcelot was so named at the fountain stone'. Since Launcelot received in baptism a name different from the one he originally used, he must have been baptised as a grown man after his own name of Launcelot was well established, for his baptismal name was not familiarly used. He was thus not born within the Christian community. We would therefore expect to find his earlier name a barbarian one, and his baptismal name to be Roman.

The word Launcelot is reminiscent of the Saxon name of Wlenca or Wlanc, meaning 'The Proud One', which was not uncommon. Lancing in Sussex is the village of the people of Wlenc (Wlencingas); Linchmore in the same county was once spelt

Wlenchemere, 'The Mere of Wlenca'; Longslow in Shropshire in the *Domesday Book* is Walanceslaw, meaning 'Wlanca's Burial Mound'; and there is a Wlencing in the *Anglo-Saxon Chronicle* who came to Britain in AD 477. Arthur may well have numbered men of Saxon or Germanic descent among his officers. So that Launcelot may be a form invented by a French copyist for an original Wlanca, a German or Saxon. Such a man, heathen by birth, may well have been baptised when he first entered the service of Arthur. His baptismal name would have been Roman, although at first glance the name Galahad does not seem to be.

If this baptismal name featured in the lost Chronicle of Arthur, it might be reconstructed by speculating for what original name a careless or ignorant copyist could have written 'Galahad'. A likely source of error lies in the abbreviations of which the Romans made such abundant use and which would have been unfamiliar to later clerks. The last syllable, HAD, immediately recalls the abbreviation of Hadrian, a name familiar and re-vered in Britain which could well have been chosen as a baptismal name. GALA also recalls an Emperor's name, Galerius, after whom one of the two consular provinces of Britain has been named. An abbreviated written form of GAL. HAD for Galerius Hadrianus might easily have given rise to the name of Galahad. In a declining society men look towards the great names of the past: the name Constantine echoes continually throughout the period; Ambrosius bore the name of a famous Emperor, Aure-lianus. It would have been natural and fashionable for the Ger-manic officer to take his baptismal names from two Emperors whose fame lived on in Britain, Galerius who had given his name to a province, and Hadrian who had built the Wall.

So Wlanca the heathen became Galerius Hadrianus the Christ-ian, whose names were abbreviated in some lost chronicle to GAL. HAD. In his lifetime he continued to be known by his original name of Wlanca which, in the French romances, became Launcelot. His son Galahad later occupied the Siege Perilous, be-coming (if our deductions are correct) governor of the province of Maxima Caesariensis, named after the Galerius from whom his own name was derived.

According to Malory, Galahad was the son of Launcelot by Elaine, daughter of one of the rulers of Britain and descended from Joseph of Arimathea. No doubt her name was Helena and, whether or not she was a direct descendant of Joseph, the story suggests that she was a member of a Christian family that had long been resident in the island. Many of the stories link Galahad with Joseph, his famous ancestor. If Joseph had come to Britain as the legends tell us, there is no reason to doubt that he left descendants and that these would have been proud to record their ancestry. With this background Galahad would have been typical of the new inhabitants of Britain : his father Germanic and his mother descended from a man who came from one of the eastern provinces of the old Empire. This was the kind of descent which the old mixture of immigrant and ex-serviceman, with the added dash of Saxon blood, had made typical of the island.

Of Launcelot himself the legends tell a strange story. Although Malory shows him as a friend and defender of Arthur, he is also the lover of Arthur's wife Guenever and it is this love that finally breaks the fellowship of the Round Table, and leads to the death of Arthur. In the last episode of Malory's story, Launcelot and his followers follow Mordred and oppose Arthur. The Germanic Wlanca finally finds a place with his own kin and, after Arthur's death, returns to his home on the Continent. He is clearly a foreign soldier whose roots were never in Britain, following Arthur for a while, but finally returning to his own folk.

If the story of Launcelot and Guenever also comes from some lost Chronicle of Arthur—and Malory is unlikely to have invented it totally—its original form may be surmised. It is unlikely that such a chronicle, concerned with the battles and political activities of the Duke of Britain, would have devoted any considerable space to a mere love story; to do so would have been untypical of chronicles of like date and nature. The story of Guenever must originally have had some political significance to give it a place.

The V or W of other languages was transcribed by British clerks as Gu. If this has happened to the name of Arthur's wife, we have a name like Wenever or Winiver. Now Winifred or Winifrith is a good Saxon name, and though philologically Guenever and Winifred cannot be related, the one could derive from the other in the writings of men not familiar with Saxon names, who were trying to adapt them to British writing and spelling.

If so, and if Arthur's wife was in fact of Saxon descent, then political results worthy of a place in the lost chronicle might well have flowed from the marriage. If Arthur's marriage had been an attempt to consolidate a peace between the Britons and the English, his chronicler would certainly have mentioned it. Perhaps the marriage failed in its purpose and, when war broke out afresh, Arthur sent Guenever back to her own people. He could have chosen no more suitable escort than his Germanic officer Wlanca. The event would have been worthy of record, and maybe the romance and love story, with Launcelot's improbable betrayal of his friend and leader, has its origin in the departure of Wlanca and Winifred, by Arthur's orders, back to her own people before the new battles were fought. A political act thus became an improbable romance.

There are slight traces of some such story to be found in other sources than Malory. In the *Life of St Gildas* Arthur is shown besieging Glastonbury because he is separated from his wife. In this version she is called Guenuver. In one of the Welsh Triads is the fantastic story that Arthur married three wives in succession, each called Gwenhwyvar (here the syllables more closely approximate to Winifred). The number of Arthur's wives can be discounted, since all the Triads show events in groups of three, but the strange story itself cannot be dismissed. Might it not be trying to record that Arthur put his wife away, and remarried her after a period of separation? After Wlanca led her away by Arthur's command, she and Arthur could have reunited, perhaps after his final victory, as a renewed pledge of peace.

Finally, the name of Guenever's father as given by Malory is interesting. She is said to be the daughter of King Leodegrance of Cameliard. The first part of this, 'Leode', is itself suggestive of a Saxon name. The word *leod* is Saxon, and means a people or nation, but can also mean the leader of a people; it forms part of various names, such as Leodivine and Leofric. There is a Leodwald in the *Anglo-Saxon Chronicle*, who appears in the genealogy of the kings of Northumberland under the entry for 729, as the great-grandfather of Ceolwulf who then reigned. Leodwald cannot of course be equated with Leodegrance, but here is evidence for a Saxon name of this kind existing in about 600, a mere sixty or seventy years after Arthur's death. So that Guenever's father was indeed almost certainly Saxon. In the sequence of Malory's narrative Arthur's marriage takes place after he has fought some of his campaigns, and after 'many Kings and Lords held great war against him'. He marries Guenever after consulting Merlin his counsellor, and it is after this marriage that he founded the Round Table. In terms of the Winifred story, this may indicate that Arthur after his first successes against the English made a truce, sealed by a marriage between himself and Winifred, daughter of one of the English leaders. Then, after an uneasy period, war broke out again and Winifred, escorted by Wlanca, returned to her people. Later, if the hint of the Triads is to be taken, she returned to Arthur.

Of the other knights, Sir Kay has a special place in the stories. Malory makes him foster-brother to Arthur and, in the early part of the narrative, Kay tries to seize power in Britain for himself. However, Arthur succeeds in establishing himself and appoints Kay to be 'seneschal of England'. The *Black Book* has a poem in which Kay again holds a special place. He seems to rank almost as Arthur's equal, since Arthur demands admission to a castle in the joint names of 'Arthur and worthy Chei'. In this poem he is the outstanding hero of Arthur's men, his sword cannot be taken from him, and all boasts are vain against him in battle. He is the leader of the battles, terrible in fighting, and slays as would a hundred men; he is invincible and can never be slain unless it is God's will. Both Malory and the *Black Book* seem to to describing a man of outstanding importance, possibly Arthur's second in command.

Was Kay, or Chei, or Kei, as he is variously spelt, a man like Arthur of Roman birth and background, whose real name was Caius? Was this Caius the man chosen by Arthur to fill the important post of *vicarius*? Some such appointment, not under-stood by later writers, might have given rise to Malory's descrip-tion of him, impossible to accept as it stands, as 'seneschal of England'.

There is a possible hint of the Count of Britain in the pages of Malory—Sir Baudwin of Britain, who was appointed con-stable. Here at any rate is again the shadow-figure of some high officer. The title constable itself derived from the word *comes*, and was originally *comes stabuli*, officer in charge of the stables, or marshal of cavalry. Malory gives Baudwin the significant title of Baudwin of Britain and he may indeed have held the office of count.

It is impossible now to identify each of the knights with his precise office in Arthur's council. Generally these men must have been the garrison commanders and officers of the Roman type of government which Arthur had established based on the *Notitia Dignitatum*. We glimpse the shadow of Caius, his deputy and possible *vicarius* of Britain, for in those troubled days the military title of *dux* would become the senior of the two. Some officers may have been of Germanic descent, like the Wlanca whom we have surmised. The supreme cavalry commander, Baudwin, is faintly to be seen. Was Sir Agravaine a man bearing the old name of Agrippa, with its military memories dating from the time of Augustus? Was King Marc of Cornwall in fact Marcus, a local leader, just as Sir Tristan, his kinsman, was Drustans?

So the knights can be seen stripped of their medieval plumes, in the workaday armour of fighting soldiers, sitting at council with Arthur, commanding their garrisons, completing the paperwork of their offices, victualling and arming their troops, fighting their campaigns with vigour and efficiency, the last of the Romans in Britain, and indeed the last Romans in Europe, following their general, Arthur the last champion, not without success; and leaving their mark permanently upon the composition and character of Britain and of the new British people.

AUXILIARY HORSEMAN, FROM A TOMBSTONE AT CHÂLON-SUR-SAÔNE

If in the legendary knights of Arthur we have a distorted picture of real men, of soldiers who marched and sweated, fought and froze, starved and struggled in the service of Britain, do the adversaries whom Arthur fought in the legends represent shadowy portraits of his real foes?

The curt and laconic entries of the *Anglo-Saxon Chronicle* present one dominant figure among the English during the period of Arthur's struggle. This is Cerdic, leader of the West Saxons. He came to Britain in 495 when, according to the dates that have been proposed, Arthur was about twenty-three. Ambrosius had been dead for some three years, and Uther Pendragon was leader of the Britons. The death of Ambrosius had weakened British resistance and encouraged new waves of invaders. But if Cerdic had heard in his Continental home that the Britons were leaderless, that landings could be made without danger, and that his ambitions would find easy vent, he was soon shown his error. The *Chronicle* records that he fought the Britons on the same day that he arrived with his five shiploads of followers and his son, Cynric. The British army was still in being, and Uther Pendragon was proving a worthy successor to Ambrosius.

In 508, as already described, Cerdic and Cynric obtained a great victory and slew a British king whose name was Natanleod, together with 5,000 men. In 514 the West Saxons came to Britain and in 519 Cerdic and Cynric took over the government of that people. In the same year they fought with the Britons. In 527 they fought a further battle, and in 530 they seized the Isle of Wight. In 534, thirty-nine years after his landing in the island, Cerdic died and was succeeded by Cynric as King of the West Saxons.

From Cerdic were descended all the kings of the West Saxons. Alfred, England's darling, who 300 years later was to defend the island against the Danish invaders, was his descendant. Indeed, through the vicissitudes of the Norman conquest and all the later changes of dynasties, the kin of Cerdic has continued as the Royal House of England. Such is the amazing continuity of English history that the present Royal family are directly descended from the soldier-adventurer who, one and a half millenia ago, grounded his five ships on the shores of Britain, and fought the Britons for a precarious foothold on the hostile beaches.

His sword must have been more than once opposed to the cavalry of Arthur and their thrusting lances—at Glein or at Guinnion, or elsewhere. The *Anglo-Saxon Chronicle* is silent about British triumphs and records only the fields of Cerdic's victories. If any of Arthur's adversaries found a place in the legend we would expect to find there the figure of Cerdic or his shadow.

Before we seek him out, there are two points about him that should be more closely examined. The first is that although he has gained his place in history as King of the West Saxons, he did not lead these folk into the island, nor was he their king from the first. It was no less than nineteen years after Cerdic's first coming that the West Saxons landed, no doubt under their own leaders, and it was a further five years before Cerdic became their ruler—after he had been in Britain for twenty-four years. Since he had a grown-up son when he first came, he must have been in his sixties by the time he ruled. Though accepted as king by the West Saxons, he was not himself of their number.

The second point about Cerdic is his name, which is not Saxon. It is the same as the name Caractacus, borne by the British hero who fought the armies of Claudius 450 years before. It is the same as Ceretic, the name of Hengist's British interpreter during his negotiations with Vortigern. As Ceredig it is to be found in other writings concerning the Britons. The writer of the *Anglo-Saxon Chronicle*, setting down a name which was foreign and unfamiliar to him, has simply omitted a vowel between the *r* and the *d*, and Ceredig or Ceredic has become Cerdic.

Here is an extraordinary fact—that Cerdic the great war leader of the English, founder of the English monarchy and progenitor of the great procession of English kings, bore the British name of Caradoc or its then equivalent, and seems therefore to have been of British blood.

Logic and coherence can now be seen in the story told in the *Anglo-Saxon Chronicle*. Cerdic was not himself one of the West Saxons, but took their government into his hands late in his career, either by invitation or by conquest. He himself, and his son Cynric, arrived before the West Saxons, and quite independently of them. He was not a native of Britain, since he came as an invader, yet his name suggests that he was British by descent. Geoffrey Ashe *(From Caesar to Arthur)* suggests that Cerdic came from the region near the mouth of the Loire, for here was an area where Britons and Saxons lived close together; and there were other regions where men of the two races were living side by side, in Brittany for example. When Cerdic came to Britain he was accompanied by his son whose name, Cynric, may well be Saxon. So it may be that, before he came with his war band to the island, Cerdic or Caradoc (as we may more properly call him), had married a Saxon wife from some neighbouring family, and had given a Saxon name to his son.

Some time after the death of Ambrosius he heard of the unsettled state of Britain, and of the opportunities for establishing himself in the land of his ancestors. He gathered a troop of followers, men of his own race and men of his wife's folk together, and sailed in five ships to Britain. His landing was opposed by the Britons, and it was this incident that constrained him to throw in his lot with the English rather than with his own people. He became one of their leaders and for his war prowess was finally acclaimed King of the West Saxons.

It is therefore this figure, Caradoc from Gaul, who was the chief adversary of Arthur and who must be sought in the pages of fable. We find him in *Morte d'Arthur* (Chapter VIII of Book I), thinly disguised as the King of Carados, or King Carados, who came to Arthur early in the latter's reign with 500 knights. At first, according to Malory, Arthur thought that King Carados came in friendship, 'for he weened that all the kings and knights had come for great love, and to have done him worship at his feast'. Arthur made great joy, and sent great presents.

> But King Carados and his associates would none receive, but rebuked the messenger shamefully, and said they had no joy to receive no gifts of a beardless boy that was come of low blood, and sent him word they would none of his gifts, but that they were come to give him gifts with hard swords betwixt the neck and the shoulders.

King Carados also said that 'it was great shame to all of them to see such a boy to have a rule of so noble a realm as this land was'.

Two facts here accord with our ideas of Cerdic : the first that Carados was originally believed by Arthur to be a friend; the second that Arthur was very young. When Caradoc first landed the Britons may well have thought that he came as a friend, since he was a kinsman of theirs. Moreover in that year, 495, Arthur (according to the dates already discussed) was a young man of about twenty-three. Malory's narrative may echo the precise words of some negotiations and argument that took place. Cerdic probably came hoping to make common cause with the Britons and to find opportunities of command with them. Perhaps he was confronted, on landing, by the young Arthur, Uther Pendragon's second in command. The ambition of the one and the youth of the other could have been among the causes of the clash that followed, which resulted in Caradoc fighting the Britons on the very day he landed; Caradoc found there was no room for him among the Britons, and no hope of displacing the proud and dedicated young leader of their army.

Why has the name of Caradoc suffered yet another change in Malory's pages to appear as Carados? There is a simple explanation. During the latter period of the Roman Empire, under the influence of Constantinople, the Greek alphabet came to be mingled with the Roman. In the Greek alphabet the letter Sigma (S) had a capital form C, easily confused with the Roman C. On the provincial coins of Probus and Carus, the names of these Emperors were written ΠPOBOC and KAPOC. The letters O C represented the sound OS and corresponding to the Latin ending US. To a scribe familiar with the two alphabets, Roman and Greek, the name Caradoc, lacking, as did all barbarian names, the classical ending of US or OS, might well have been taken to be Carados, as being more correct and more capable of grammatical inflection. Again we see the shadow of a lost Chronicle of Arthur; and now we see it composed or copied by a scribe of shaky scholarship who was trying to read into a barbarian name a Graeco-Roman form.

Malory's description of Arthur's first war numbers King

Carados among his adversaries. If this account contains some true tradition, then the battle of the River Glein took place some time after 495, that is to say after the coming of Caradoc. Malory says that before this engagement, some of the followers of Carados deserted to join Arthur 'and that comforted him greatly'. So Carados was left alone with his Saxon soldiers, irrevocably committing him to the English cause. In Malory's description of Arthur's second battle (which may be the battle on the river Dubglass), King Carados again figures. On this occasion he is almost slain, and is rescued by one of his allies.

Carados finally vanishes from the pages of Malory, killed by Launcelot. Book XX relates how Launcelot remembered him as 'a noble knight, and a passing strong man'; Launcelot counted his defeat of Carados among his greatest triumphs and saw it as an especial reason why he should have 'Arthur's good grace', even after he and Arthur had parted company, and civil war had broken out between them. Cerdic was a man worthy to be the chief adversary of Arthur, Duke of Britain, and to be ancestor to the English kings.

As parts of Malory's tales thus coincide with known facts, it is worth enquiring whether other parts of his story contain historical facts which are not obtainable elsewhere. A character worth examining from this point of view is King Ban of Benwick, brother of King Bors.

King Ban's name is so remarkably close to the name of his kingdom that it leads to the suspicion that 'King Ban of Benwick' is a little like 'Bishop Eborius of York', recorded as having attended a conference of bishops at Arles in AD 314. The Latin name for York was Eboracum, and the Archbishop of York signs himself *Ebor* to this day. Some chronicler going through the records of the conference, or a later copyist, mistook the name of the bishop's see, or the bishop's signature, for the name of the bishop, and the name of Eborius, Bishop of York, entered history.

We have already seen that 'the King of Carados' is later referred to as King Carados, showing confusion between the man's own name and that of his territory. If a similar error lies at the origin of King Ban of Benwick, his territory might have been variously spelled Ban or Ben, and the ending *wick* may not have been part of the name of his kingdom. Malory duly suggests where this kingdom is to be found, but the story and background he supplies for Ban should be considered first. Arthur's first war showed that his enemies were exceedingly strong; besides the support of Carados, they had the help of other leaders. Therefore Merlin told Arthur : 'There are two brethren beyond the sea, and they be kings both and marvellous good men of their hands; and that one hight King Ban of Benwick, and that other hight King Bors of Gaul, that is France.' Merlin explained that Ban and Bors were at war in their own country with a king named Claudas. Arthur was accordingly advised to

> send unto the kings Ban and Bors by two trusty knights with letters well devised, that if they will come and see King Arthur and his court, and so help him in his wars, that he will be sworn unto them to help them in their wars against King Claudas.

Two of Arthur's men crossed into Gaul, helped Ban and Bors in their wars, and brought the two kings to Britain with 300 men, and with their brother Gwenbaus who was a 'wise clerk'. Two of Arthur's men kept guard in Gaul over the lands of Ban and Bors while the two kings stayed with Arthur as allies. In Arthur's next battle, fought against a confederation from the North, Ban and Bors played a leading part. Bors nearly slew Carados and both were continually with Arthur in the fighting. They were with Arthur when he went to the rescue of Leodegrance, father of Guenever. Afterwards they returned to their own country. All this is in Malory's first book. Years later (in Book IV) Merlin himself visited Benwick, and there met the boy Launcelot, son of Ban's wife, Elaine. Launcelot grew up and came to Arthur's court but, after many adventures and after his final quarrel with Arthur, returned to Benwick, to become king of all the lands that had belonged to Claudas, his father's enemy. This was in the dark and unhappy time when Arthur's fellowship was breaking up, and not long before the last battle of Camlann. Malory (in Chapter III of his twentieth book) says that Launcelot 'sailed unto Benwick; some men call it Bayonne, and some men call it Beaune, where the wine of Beaune is.'

Behind this story lurk events not elsewhere recorded but hinted at in the story of Wlanca. Not all the longships crossing the Channel in those troubled days were laden with the enemies of Britain. The Saxons were not the only travellers to watch their ship's prow rise and dip as they drew towards new dangers and new opportunities in the island of Britain. From Gaul there also came friends to Arthur, Ban of Benwick and his brother Bors; and there came to his service some who had earlier settled in Gaul, Briton and Saxon, Celt and German, exile and adventurer. Some like Caradoc came with no certain loyalty but seeking to create kingdoms for themselves, whether peopled by their own kin or by strangers. Over the Channel too there passed ships of Arthur's, taking his messengers and embassies to the new kingdoms in Gaul, offering treaties, alliances and protection in return for reinforcements. The story of Ban of Benwick brings home to us the complexity of the struggle for Britain, and the resources and wide sweep of Arthur's government.

That he was father or kinsman of Launcelot, or Wlanca, suggests that the King of Benwick was of Germanic origin. Like Cerdic, he would have come from a place where Germans and Saxons were settled in Gaul. As already mentioned, this had happened in the region round the Loire, and the search for Benwick may need to go no further than Beaune, as Malory himself suggests. Beaune lies some eighty miles from the river Loire and its early spelling was Belna. In a document of the Merovingian period it appears as Belenum Castrum, showing its Roman origin in a camp or fortified place. The place where a group of houses and shops was built outside a military fort was classified as a *vicus*, and such a settlement close to the Roman camp of Belna or Belenum might well have become known as Belnae Vicus or

Beleni Vicus. There is no record of such a spelling for Beaune but similar forms are recorded elsewhere. If in the lost chronicle Belnae Vicus or some modified form such as Belnevicus or Benevicus appeared, it is easy to see how, in the hands of a copyist familiar with English place names, the legendary town of Benwick came to be born.

Beaune was the capital of a separate and semi-independent country attached to the kingdom of the Burgundians. The latter, members of the eastern branch of the German race, had come as refugees into Gaul some time after AD 411. The great Aetius (to whom the Britons had in vain appealed for help) had defeated them in 435 with a mixed army of Visigoths, Saxons and a few Burgundians who turned against their fellow countrymen. The Burgundians retained their king, but shortly afterwards they were attacked by the terrible Attila and their kingdom was almost destroyed. The Romans took advantage of this disaster to their former enemies and settled them as Treaty Troops on the banks of the Rhone, in the Saône basin, and along the upper reaches of the Loire. No doubt other foreign troops who had served in this region were similarly settled, including Visigoths and Saxons from the armies of Aetius. The kingdom of Burgundy, essentially Germanic in population, was legally established, founded (as was the English kingdom in Britain) upon a settlement of Treaty Troops. But the kingdom was short-lived. In 516 died the last of her great kings, Gundebad. The Franks absorbed Burgundy into the Frankish state and she later became one of the most powerful vassals of the crown of France. The Frankish conqueror was King Clovis, supported by other princes of his dynasty, Clodomer and Clothair.

Malory writes that the King of Benwick was at war in his own country with a king named Claudas. It is not impossible to hear in this legendary struggle some echo of the real struggle between the Burgundian region of Beaune and Clodomer the Frank. Again this may be a story from a lost Chronicle of Arthur, and may represent the shadow of historical fact. A leader from

Beaune, after the death of Gundebad, was defeated by Clodomer and sought a new life and perhaps a new kingdom overseas. The Burgundians, for all their barbarian origins, now saw themselves as Romans and their struggle with the Franks as a fight between citizens and barbarians. Although with the triumph of Clodomer and his colleagues their struggle had ended in failure, the same struggle was still being carried on by Arthur in Britain. Across the Channel there were fields where the battles that had been lost in Burgundy might be re-fought and possibly won.

So the leader of Beaune, with a troop of 300 followers and kinsmen, of mixed Burgundian, Visigoth and Saxon stock, took ship and came to Britain. There on the shores of Tribruit, and on the hill of Badon, they helped in Rome's last stand against the barbarians. These battles fought in the northern mists were remote from the seven hills of Rome and far from their own vineyards; yet they were none the less the last rearguard actions of the Eternal City. The men from Beaune were unwilling to accept that Rome was defeated while the armies of Britain stood, and while the Christian cause, however tenuously, still held out in the northern island.

XI

FROM DUKE TO KING

I F Arthur was indeed Duke of Britain, a military leader who commanded the armies of the kings of Britain but who himself had no royal title, the question arises as to how the title of king became attached to his name. In his lifetime the Roman designations of duke and count, of consul and tribune, were growing archaic and their meanings becoming blurred. Throughout Europe the new kingdoms were replacing the old provinces and dioceses and the title of king was becoming the only familiar and accustomed designation of power. Arthur, in a valiant endeavour to keep alive the Roman traditions of Britain had, like Ambrosius before him, striven to give fresh meanings to the old forms. But even to his contemporaries the title of king was more easily understood, and sprang more easily to men's lips, than the fading title of Duke of Britain.

When Roman rule faded in the island, the old kingly families of the tribes and regions re-emerged. Four hundred years of Roman rule had not caused the States of Britain to forget that once they were ruled by kings. The English brought kings with them, and gave a new strength to the institution of kingship. With the English the sword and the sceptre were one, and the crown itself was a war-helmet. There was fresh cause to equate leadership, especially military leadership, with kingship.

While Arthur lived, and while his purpose and methods were clear, his own people no doubt accepted him as leader of the army, commander of the troops from all the kingdoms of the Roman Island, successor to the great Ambrosius, and Duke of Britain. Even so, in some of the remoter parts where he was known only by repute as the great leader and victor over the invaders, he may even in his lifetime have been thought of as a king. His English enemies who knew little of Roman titles would certainly have considered him a king. To them, all military leaders of his stature—like Hengist, Octha his son, and Cerdic— were kings.

As mentioned in Chapter VIII, Nennius in making the oldest recorded mention of Arthur writes that he fought together with the kings of Britain but that he himself was the *Dux Bellorum.* Once he was dead, his triumphs remembered but his purpose forgotten, popular acclamation gave him a title he never bore in his lifetime.

The work ascribed to Nennius contains, besides the *History of the Britons* from which quotations have been made, a section entitled *De Mirabilibus Britanniae,* or *The Marvels of Britain.* This lists marvellous and miraculous tales collected from various parts of the island. One is about a heap of stones which, however often it is removed, miraculously renews itself; one of the stones on the heap is marked with the footprint of the dog Cabal which belonged to Arthur. The story itself tells us little but the words used to describe Cabal as Arthur's dog tell much. '*Cabal,*' writes Nennius, '*qui erat canis Arthuri militis.*' That is to say, Cabal was the dog of Arthur the soldier. Arthur is remembered simply as a military leader. Another of the marvels is the grave of Anir, said to be a son of Arthur whom Arthur himself slew and buried. Again the words used are '*Arthuri militis*', or Arthur the soldier. This section is later in date than the chapters of the *History of the Britons* dealing with Arthur's battles, and Arthur's memory is now moving into the era of marvel and myth. Yet the work is of respectable antiquity, and we see Arthur becoming a legend before he ever becomes a king, and before his true position had been quite forgotten.

Gildas too is a significant witness on this point even though he does not mention Arthur by name. Immediately after describing the victory of Badon and the sorry times that followed, he goes on to rebuke the kings of Britain. 'Britain has kings,' he writes, 'but they are tyrants.' Then he charges them all with robbery, injustice, fornication, adultery, perjury and a host of other sins, and proceeds to mention five of them by name. One of them, Maglocunnus, is reproved for murder, homosexuality

ROMAN HELMET, FROM STATUE OF HADRIAN FOUND AT COPRANO

(he is 'soaked in the wine of the sodomitical grape'), for incest and for other evil-doings; yet his military virtues are recognised. Gildas calls him 'more generous than others in giving, but more reckless in sinning; valiant in arms, but more mighty in working out thy soul's destruction.'

Gildas gives a comprehensive account of the faults, and at least touches on the virtues, of the island's kings. It is unlikely that Arthur, had he been one of them, would have been excluded from the contemporary catalogue, whatever the writer's opinion of him.

The early Welsh poems, written in an area where the traditions and memories of Arthur lingered longest, do not call him king. The poem from the *Black Book* already quoted in the context of Arthur's death, refers simply to the grave 'of Arthur', with no title at all. A poem called 'Godeddin' written, probably by Aneurin, within eighty years or so of Arthur's death, also mentions him without any title; so do the Welsh Triads. One of the poems in the *Black Book* gives him a title that is as surprising as it is unusual. The poem is called 'Gereint, Son of Erbin', and in it Arthur is described, in the Welsh language, as *Arthur . . . ameraudur*, Arthur the Emperor. The last word is the Welsh form of the Latin *Imperator*. Either the poet conceived Arthur as having taken supreme power in Britain, as had Carausius, Constantine and Maximus before him, with the title of Roman Emperor, or he was using the word *Imperator* in its original sense of commander in chief, and was accurately describing Arthur's position. In either case, the poet was aware of the Roman tradition which Arthur was following, and is telling us clearly that Arthur was known to have used Roman designations; he is shown as the soldier in transition. He is becoming something more than a soldier or a simple commander. But the *dux* of Nennius, the *miles* of the *Marvels of Britain*, and the simple name of Arthur in the earliest Welsh poems, make it clear that he was not known as king to his own people.

The earliest document to speak of Arthur as king is the *Life of St Gildas*, written at Llancarfan in Ireland, the earliest extant manuscript of which is of the fourteenth century. The tone of this work shows that it was first written down before Arthur had acquired the reputation of blameless perfection. There are traces of the hostility that undoubtedly existed between Gildas and Arthur, and evidence of long-forgotten tensions and differences between Arthur and some of his other contemporaries. Some of the disruptive forces that brought about the civil war in which

Arthur died have left their vestiges in the narrative. Arthur, as we have seen, is shown as having slaughtered Hueil, who was a hero to the writers of the tale, 'a devoted warrior and most famous soldier', 'a great-minded youth', and 'a most victorious youth, the best of men, whom the inhabitants spoke of hopefully as their future king'. Here then is Arthur as his enemies in Britain saw him: ruthless, ambitious and tolerating no rival. This is a portrait of the Arthur seen by Mordred, a man whose power had grown too great and in whom the love of power, and the fear of losing it, had bred a cruelty and tyranny that had to be destroyed.

But this was not the opinion of those many Britons who had followed him from the river Glen to the hill of Badon. Nor was it the view of posterity. Evidently, therefore, this *Life of St Gildas* was written fairly soon after Arthur's death, before the golden legend had obliterated the grievances of old quarrels. Significantly Arthur is described as 'the king of the whole of Greater Britain', and as 'the king of Universal Britain': Britain had many kings but Arthur was holding some special position of power in relation to the whole island. When the book was written the only word known to describe this outstanding office was that of king. The titles of *dux* and of *comes* were fading and the leader became known as King Arthur. In the medieval world, where the throne had finally replaced the Roman curule chair, and where kingship was the sole institution of power, this was inevitable.

One title from the ancient world remained, the title of *tyrannus* or tyrant. In the Greek this originally meant quite simply 'king', but it had come to be reserved for the worst aspects of arbitrary and despotic kingship. The author of the *Life of St Gildas* writes of 'Arthur the tyrant', seeming to echo the resentment and mistrust of Arthur's power that led to the field of Camlann. Again we are shown Arthur as Mordred saw him and as he appeared to his enemies in the civil war. Alternatively this title of tyrant may be an echo of another event for which we have no proof and which, if it ever occurred, is now totally forgotten except in that single word. The designation of tyrant in the fourth and fifth centuries was applied to men who, with no legal right beyond the right of conquest and with no merits but ambition, had seized power and called themselves Roman Emperors. The historians spoke of the Thirty Tyrants, to describe the motley procession of illegal Emperors in the later years of the Empire. It is possible that, after Badon, Arthur was presumptuous enough to seek the revival of a higher form of power than that of leader of the armies. Did he proclaim himself Emperor, as many others had done who had never seen Rome itself, and whose title had been ratified by no higher authority than their own military success? Then to his critics and enemies he would have been Arthur the Tyrant indeed. Such an event might explain the phrase 'Arthur the Emperor' *(Arthur ameraudur)* in the *Black Book*.

But it could hardly have happened without leaving some traces in recorded history or at least some further evidence in the legends. It is far more likely that his enemies merely suspected him of the ultimate presumption, and that the epithet of tyrant is an echo of the stories and apprehensions put about by his contemporary critics.

There is no reason to doubt that in his lifetime Arthur was, as Nennius says, the *dux*, the military leader, of Britain. If he assumed or was given this formal title at a time when a copy of the *Notitia Dignitatum* was available, some of the features attaching to that office would probably be found in the stories about him.

The *Notitia Dignitatum* shows the badge of the Duke of Britain, as already noted. It is a formal heraldic depiction of an island, bearing the symbols of the towns and forts under the Duke's command (see page 8). Originally the *dux* had to watch over the North from his headquarters at York. Somewhere near, therefore, we should expect to find his army's field headquarters for northern campaigns.

South-west of York and on the main Roman road to Chester

is the village of Slack in Yorkshire, which has been identified with a Roman town named Camulodunum. (This is not to be confused with the Camulodunum in Essex, the modern Colchester.) It is mentioned in Ptolemy's *Geography* of the second century and in the seventh-century document known as the *Ravenna Cosmography*, so that it had a long record of existence. In the old British language, *dun* means a fort, and the British name would have been Camulodun, the final *um* being added by the Romans so that the word could be inflected. The laws of philology do not permit the assumption that this name could have changed to Camelot; but if it were taken by a British scribe as Camulod-dun, the fort of Camulod, then an error in copying could give Camelot or something very close.

Arthur's own territory lay in the South West, but to mark his position as Duke of Britain he would probably have continued the custom of maintaining a formal campaigning headquarters in the North. His garrison commanders in the area would have made it their centre when they were visited from time to time by the *Dux*. These visits would have been notable events, and Malory's story shows that Arthur's visits to Camelot were in fact rare and special occasions of state. Here, then, may be the Camelot of the legends.

There are other claimants to the name of Camelot—one of course being Cadbury Castle in Somerset. Ever since the fifteenth century there has been a strong belief that this was once Arthur's famous city. But the ascription seems to rest on an early identification of the river Camel with Geoffrey of Monmouth's 'river Cambula' and on the village named Camel that lie near Cadbury Castle. In fact, Geoffrey's reference is probably to the fort of Camboglanna on the Wall, where Arthur fought his last battle. Recent excavations have shown evidence of sixth-century occupation at Cadbury. But whether this occupation was by Arthur is quite another matter. (See also page 198).

Wherever Camelot may have been, many lines of evidence converge to suggest that Arthur was Duke of Britain. But since he was the last man in Britain to hold a Roman title, obstinately and bravely trying to continue the forms of order in a time of chaos, it is not surprising, in the dark times that followed, when his motives were forgotten and the forms he had used were dead, that men sought a new name to describe him. So Arthur, Duke of Britain, became King Arthur, the hero of the whole island, of English and Britons alike.

XII

THE SWORDS AND THE GRAIL

WOVEN into the legends of Arthur are many miraculous elements which at first sight appear to be entirely fabulous and which seem to diminish the credibility of the whole story. Chief among these are the recurrent themes of Arthur's magical swords and of the Holy Grail. But just as the knights in the legends may be the figures of real personages, distorted by time and by error, so these two themes may be shadows of real events, linked with the historical Arthur and with Britain's last stand against the English.

In Malory's story there are two swords of Arthur. The first of these was the sword which he drew out of a stone, by which miracle his leadership was recognised or by which, in Malory's words, he became King of England. Immediately afterwards he appointed Kay as seneschal of all England, and Baudwin of Britain was made constable, and Ulfius was made chamberlain; 'and Sir Brastias was made warden to wait upon the north from Trent forwards, for it was at that time the most part of the king's enemies.'

In this passage the threads of truth and fiction seem completely intertwined. The appointment of officers, and the prosaic statement, known to be true, that Arthur had many enemies in the North, seem authentic and factual. But the sword drawn from the stone is the very stuff of legend. Since it is so closely woven with factual statements it is sensible to enquire whether the story of the sword in the stone may itself have some basis in fact.

Malory relates that after the death of Uther Pendragon the succession remained in doubt, and the country in great danger. Merlin and the Archbishop of Canterbury gathered all the great ones of the land together in London. In the greatest church of London, Mass was celebrated and

> there was seen in the churchyard, against the high altar, a great stone four-square, like unto a marble stone, and in the midst thereof was like an anvil of steel a foot on high, and therein stuck a fair sword naked by the point.

Written round the sword, in letters of gold, were words predicting that whoever pulled out the sword 'should be king of all England'. Many tried and failed. The young Arthur, unaccountably omitting to read the letters of gold, pulled out the sword when all had departed, simply because he needed a sword for his foster-brother, Kay. After an attempted deception by Kay, Arthur pulled out the sword again in the presence of witnesses, proving his right to succeed Uther Pendragon and to take the leadership of Britain. Malory makes it clear that he himself did not invent the tale, for he mentions a French book from which he took it.

If this part of the narrative is drawn from the lost Chronicle of Arthur, that chronicle, written in Latin, would have contained some such sentence as follows:

Arthur gladium ex saxo eripuit.
Arthur drew (or snatched away) a sword from the stone *(ex saxo)*.

Could these be a mistaken copy of other similar words, recording an authentic fact? The words that arouse suspicion are *ex saxo*, from a stone, so similar to *ex saxono*, meaning 'from a Saxon'. By substituting this version the tale becomes credible: Arthur snatched away a sword from a Saxon warrior. The capture of such a sword would have been a notable and encouraging event, and might well have been a factor in Arthur's promotion to the leadership.

Medieval clerks were accustomed to omit the letter *n*, and to show that omission by a stroke written above the word, so that the words *ex Saxono* might have been written *ex Saxoō*, or *ex Saxō*. To copy this without the horizontal line above the *o* would have been the slightest slip. From a scribe who could make the error which gave rise to Carados it would be not unexpected. Moreover the English very soon called themselves *Angli*, or Englishmen, and the name Saxon came to be forgotten. It survived only among their enemies. To the Welsh and the Scots the Englishman is a Saxon (Saesneg or Sassenach) to this day. To an Englishman, copying an old Latin manuscript of British or Welsh origin, the word *Saxō* would not immediately have recalled the name of his people; it would have first been read as 'stone' or 'rock'. Arthur's victory, from which he brought home the proud trophy of a Saxon's sword, dwindles into an incredible miracle on to which later romancers both in France and England embroidered their fanciful details—the letters of gold, Kay's deception, and the ultimate triumph of Arthur. Perhaps the two threads of fact and invention are not so hard to disentangle in this story.

After Uther's death no one of his successors stood out as the obvious candidate for supreme command. Arthur, although a kinsman of Uther, was young and his career not yet so eminent as to advance his claim beyond doubt. Kay, or Caius, a soldier of great merit and reputation, was also in the running. Then Arthur led his troops against a detachment of the enemy. The engagement itself may have been of little importance but the result was dramatic, Arthur wresting away the sword of his chief adversary. This victory, and his trophy, won him the leadership. Shortly thereafter he appointed four officers to hold authority under him, the foremost being Kay who had himself been considered for the command. If this was a move to secure Kay's support, it succeeded; Kay served Arthur loyally and well for many years.

The second sword of Arthur is the more famous: Excalibur,

the miraculous weapon which he received from the Lady of the Lake. As Malory tells the story, Arthur lost the services of the men from Benwick some time after his third battle. They assisted him in the rescue of Leodegrance, father of Guenever, and then 'took their leave to go into their own countries, for King Claudas did great destruction on their lands'. Shortly afterwards Arthur's first sword was broken in battle. Merlin took him 'to a lake, the which was a fair water and broad, and in the midst of the lake Arthur was aware of an arm clothed in white samite, that held a fair sword in that hand.' A maiden then appeared and granted Arthur the gift of the sword, in return for a service to be rendered later. In his description of these events (Chapter XXV of Book I) Malory does not mention the sword's name which is given merely in the chapter heading; neither Merlin nor Arthur call it anything but 'the sword'. It is only later, in Book II, that the maiden who gave Arthur the sword, in claiming the service she had asked, calls it Excalibur, which is said to mean 'Cut-steel'. Later the sword was stolen from Arthur and in another's hands almost slew him, but it was restored to him by an enchantment of the damosel of the lake and he conquered. The end of the story is well known. Arthur, dying of his wounds after the battle of Camlann, ordered Bedevere to return it to the lake. Bedevere, after twice deceiving Arthur by hiding the sword, finally cast it far into the water; and, writes Malory in Chapter V of his Book XXI, 'there came an arm above the water and met it, and caught it, and so shook it thrice and brandished, and then vanished away the hand with the sword in the water.'

Through the story of this sword, water is a constant theme. It came to Arthur from the surface of the lake, a gift from the Lady of the Lake. When he lost it, it was restored to him by the damosel of the lake, and after his last battle it was returned by one of his followers to the waters of the lake.

The name Excalibur is not likely to have been invented. If it is a genuine survival from an ancient and authentic tradition, it is worth examining in detail. Geoffrey of Monmouth, writing about the middle of the twelfth century, before Malory, gives the name in a slightly different form; he calls it 'Caliburn', and writes of Arthur 'girding on his Caliburn, which was an excellent sword made in the Isle of Avallon.' (The Isle of Avalon, too, is a place associated with water.) He also describes Arthur's battle with Flollo, a Roman tribune. Arthur was wounded in the struggle :

> When Arthur saw his coat of mail and shield red with blood, he was inflamed with still greater rage, and lifting up his Caliburn with his utmost strength struck it through the helmet into Flollo's head, and made a terrible gash.

To reconcile the two forms of the sword's name, that portion of the name which is common to both should be isolated, omitting the additional syllable *ex*. *Ex* is of course the Latin word for 'out of' or 'from'. Was Arthur's sword obtained 'out of' or 'from' Calibur or Caliburn? Can this second part of the name be interpreted as describing whence the sword came?

The first element looks very like the old British word *cale* meaning a river or brook. This has survived unchanged both in Somerset and Dorset, as the name of a small river. It would have been one of the words used by Arthur and his contemporaries for a river.

When the English came to the island, they took over a fairly large number of British place names, particularly for rivers: Thames, Severn, Dee, Avon, and the Cale we have mentioned, are a few. They also adopted the British names for other natural features, such as hills and woods. In some cases, they seem to have mistaken the general name for a particular one, and then added the English word on to it. For example, Bredon in Worcestershire is simply the British word *bre* meaning a hill, with the old English word *dun*, also meaning a hill, added. It is as though one of the invading English asked a native British guide what the hill was called; the Briton thinking his questioner wanted to know the British word for 'hill', told him '*bre*'. The

Englishman, thinking this to be the name of the individual hill, called it Bredun, or Brehill. The British word for wood was something like *kaito* (in modern Welsh it is *coed*): out of similar confusion the names Chetwode and Cheetwood were born.

It is known that this confusion arose at least once in the case of the word *cale*. For in the Isle of Wight there is a small stream named Caul Bourne, and on it stands the village of Calbourne, once spelt Cawelburne or Cavelburn: the British word *cale* and the English word *burn* have been combined.

Both Geoffrey and Malory maintain that Arthur's sword came from water or from a place surrounded by water; yet since the two writers use different names for the weapon, it is likely that they were drawing on two separate sources. This reinforces the probability that the common tradition of water is old and contains some central truth. If so, then the fact may well have been recorded that Arthur obtained his sword *ex cale burno*, from the stream or river Cale. If the letter *n* were omitted and the contraction of a horizontal stroke substituted, such a phrase could have given rise to both forms: the Caliburn of Geoffrey and the Excalibur of Malory. Again the lost Chronicle of Arthur seems to lie in the background, miscopied and misunderstood, but relating simply that Arthur obtained his second sword from a place on a river or stream.

Consideration of the processes by which swords were at this period produced shows that a place by a river or stream was a likely source of a good weapon. To the Romans the manufacture of steel was unknown. The iron ore was reduced by charcoal or coal in simple hearth furnaces and the resulting spongy mass was reheated and hammered to drive out the slag. From this malleable iron the blacksmith forged his sword blades, and then tempered them by alternate heating and cooling. This involved not only annealing (allowing the metal to cool slowly), but quenching, that is plunging the heated blade into water in order to chill it suddenly. The manufacture of high quality swords would have been close to a river or stream in order to have abundant water for quenching. Technically, the nature of the water certainly had no effect upon the result, yet the Romans themselves ascribed some of the merits of finished weapons to the qualities of the water. For example Spanish arms and cutlery were well known in the fifth century, and their excellence was ascribed to the use of certain waters for quenching.

Such a reputation might have been won by certain streams in Britain. Since there were no iron deposits in the Isle of Wight, the Caule Bourne already mentioned, can be excluded. But the name which survived there might once have existed elsewhere. Nor would this stream have been between Hereford and the Severn Estuary, although the iron ore of the Forest of Dean was worked in the Roman period; it is too far to the west for the meeting of Saxon and Briton, necessary to produce the mixed name, to have happened in Arthur's day. Iron was also produced during the Roman period in Lincolnshire and Northamptonshire where the ore lies close to the surface: perhaps the Caleburn, where Arthur's sword was quenched and hardened, flows under another name somewhere through the iron-ore country between Corby and the Wash, in the territory guarded by the grey walls of Lindum Colonia. After the English, the Danes came to this area, so the old place names became obliterated, and Danish and Scandinavian forms prevail.

There is one other scrap of evidence. In the poem by Chrétien de Troyes called 'Le Roman de Perceval', we are told that Sir Perceval's sword required to be mended. Perceval asked whether in fact this was possible: *'S'ele porroit estre refaite?'* He is told that he must go to the lake which is beneath the castle of Cloth-oatre, and have his sword mended by Triboët, a skilful smith who lives there. He is warned to entrust the work only to this particular smith. The poem runs:

> Oïl, mais grant paine i avroit
> Qui le voie tenir savroit
> Au lac qui est soz Clothoatre,
> La le porriez faire rebatre

Et retemprer et fair saine,
Se aventure la vos maine.
N'alez se chies Triboët non,
Un fevre qui ensi a non,
Car cil le fist et refera,
Ou jamais faite ne sera
Por home qui s'en entremete
Gardez que autres main n'i mete,
Qu'il n'en saroit venir a chief.

The sword is again associated with water : for the name of the place, Clothoatre, is no invention by Chrétien de Troyes. He has clearly taken it from an English original, the last part of the word being 'water', spelt 'oatre' by a French hand. The poet Wace (writing in the twelfth century) mentions a river Escocewater (or river of the Scots) which may be the origin of Clothoatre and one of the editors of Chrétien de Troyes (Alexander Bell, 1934), equates those two words. Then the name of the smith, Triboët, is strangely reminiscent of the name of Arthur's tenth battle, on the river Tribruit. The name of the smith may have become confused with that of the river by which he worked. Perhaps Tribruit and Clothoatre are one, and perhaps both are that Cale or river where Arthur's weapons were tempered and repaired after battle.

This reconstruction explains one part of the legend, the close link between Excalibur and a stream or lake, but it leaves unsolved the second part, the Lady of the Lake. Perhaps she is the legendary shadow of some local chieftainess or queen in whose territory lay the river and the mines. The kings and royal families of Britain continued to hold regional power. Not only kings but queens were traditionally accepted as rulers; the island had already produced a Cartimandua and a Boudica. In return for the service of military leadership and assistance against the invaders, a queen may have granted Arthur the gift of his sword and of the local iron industry itself. This would explain the service demanded of Arthur by the maiden in return for the sword.

The search for Excalibur, the miraculous sword, leads away

from miracles into everyday topography, from fairyland into the
ore-fields of Northamptonshire and Lincolnshire. It indicates one
of Arthur's main preoccupations: the arming and supplying of
his troops. He had to foster and defend the local centres manu-
facturing weapons. The Forest of Dean was safe, deep in the
West, but the Lincolnshire and Northamptonshire ore deposits

A ROMAN SWORD. SKETCH BASED ON A SWORD FOUND IN THE
RIVER THAMES AND NOW IN THE BRITISH MUSEUM

were close to his frontier with the English. Excalibur was not
merely his weapon. It is a symbol of Arthur's dangers and of his
answers to those dangers. With the sword he fought and defended
the place where the sword was made. Tribruit might have been
the battle for one of the vital regions of Britain's resistance—
the area where good swords were shaped and tempered, plunged
red hot into the hissing Cale of Tribruit, to be hardened and
made ready for the defence of the Christian cause against the
barbarians.

The story of the Grail is closely linked by Malory with the story of Galahad, and through Galahad with Joseph of Arimathea.

Through his mother Elaine, daughter of King Pelles and 'cousin nigh unto Joseph of Arimathie', Galahad traced his descent directly from Joseph. It is when his father Launcelot meets Pelles and Elaine (in Malory's Book XI) that we first see the Sangreal or Holy Grail, here described as a simple vessel of gold to which the king kneeled devoutly. Nothing is mentioned of its origins or miraculous powers. King Pelles says of it : 'This is the richest thing that any man hath living.' He also prophesies (and this is significant) that 'When this thing goeth about, the Round Table shall be broken.' Later in the same book and in Book CII we are told of its powers to heal wounds and to cure the sick.

In Book XIII, when Galahad is grown to manhood and after he is led to the Siege Perilous, the vacant place at Arthur's Round Table, various of Arthur's followers go in search of the Grail, which (in Book XIX) is ultimately found by Galahad. To him there appears a vision of Jesus Christ, who reveals the origin of the Grail : 'Son, notest thou what I hold betwixt my hands? . . . This is the holy dish wherein I ate the lamb on Sher-Thursday' (i.e. Maundy Thursday). There is also a miraculous and blood-stained spear which, like the Grail itself, has power to cure. After achieving the Grail, Galahad is acclaimed king and shortly thereafter dies. The Grail and the spear are lifted into heaven by a mysterious hand : 'Sithen was there never man so hardy to say that he had seen the Sangreal.'

After this, the shadows descend upon Arthur and his companions, and events move swiftly to the final tragedy. The company of the Round Table is broken, and the last battle is fought at Camlann, where Arthur is defeated by his former comrades.

The essential elements of the story are the existence of the dish believed to have been used by Christ at the Last Supper and of the miraculous spear; association of these objects with Joseph of Arimathea; a search for the Grail; its discovery by Galahad; its final disappearance; and the linking of the Grail with the bitter division among the Companions of Arthur and with the last struggle between them. A feature is that the Grail is revealed only at intervals, its display being a mysterious and formal matter. In *Le Roman de Perceval* (Perceval being one of the knights who sought the Grail), Chrétien de Troyes records how the Grail is carried in procession with many candles, and how it is decor-ated with precious stones. This element in the story suggests an actual relic contained in a golden reliquary, solemnly and rever-ently displayed on certain occasions, carried in procession and with due ceremony shown to the assembled congregation. The story is also much concerned with the loss of the relic at some point. Its loss and subsequent recovery immediately preceded and were in some way connected with the civil war between Mordred and Arthur.

The central core of the Grail tradition does not bear the mark of invention; too much is omitted and too much left to inference. An invented story would have been more sequential and, like any artifact, would have shown a regularity and symmetry which are lacking. Chrétien de Troyes makes no mention of Joseph of Arimathea. Malory, in introducing the theme, does so almost in passing, and gives no account, as a story-teller might, of the Grail's origin. It is as though we are being given disjointed frag-ments of some tale now lost. There is no need to doubt that behind the legend lurks a real and material relic, and an account of real and material events.

The tradition that Joseph of Arimathea came to Britain and built the Old Church at Glastonbury, dedicated to the Virgin Mary, has been noted. With him, according to the legend, he brought the cup used by Christ at the Last Supper and, in some versions of the story, the spear that pierced his side. In Malory's version the Grail seems to be not a drinking cup but a platter or dish, from which Christ ate the Paschal lamb the night before the Crucifixion. ('This is the holy dish wherein I ate the lamb on

Sher-Thursday.') After Galahad has achieved the Grail, it is used in the service of communion, and Galahad takes from it the bread which has been blessed. The spear with its miraculous drops of blood is used in the same ceremony.

Even if this most sacred object had been brought to Britain, or was thought to have been conveyed there, why should it feature in the story of Arthur, and why should the traditions of a military commander be so bound up with traditions of a miracle-working relic? The reason is not hard to find. He bore Christian emblems as his ensign. He was not merely a military leader but an avowedly Christian one, the Christian faith being one of the tools with which he bound Britain into unity, and with which he opposed the forces of local loyalties, local apathies, and local ambitions.

Moreover, his way of life, his possessions, and his forms of worship would have been governed by the circumstances of his position as Duke of Britain. And there are good reasons for presuming it likely that a Duke of Britain would have possessed and guarded some supremely sacred relic.

In 1959-60, an excavation was made of the palace of the governor of the Roman province of Cyrenaica in North Africa. An account of the excavation has been published by Richard Goodchild in *Antiquity*, XXXIV, 1960. It is estimated that this palace was built nearer AD 500 than 450. It was therefore in occupation by the local *dux* at about the time that Arthur was *dux* in Britain. Cyrenaica was still in close touch with Constantinople, capital of the Eastern Empire, in a way that Britain was not, and the Duke of Britain might not have lived in the same style as the Duke of Cyrenaica. But the two offices were similar, and their administrative procedures and ceremonial would not have been unlike. (As an instance that some uniformity existed between East and West, the palace of Cyrenaica in Africa has points of similarity with the palace of Ravenna.) Arthur's residence, within the limits of his resources—isolated as he now was from Continental supplies and wealth—would have had some essential features in common with other palaces of commanders of similar standing and with the one excavated in North Africa.

The palace of the Dukes of Cyrenaica was patently both the residence and the public offices of a Christian governor. A large audience hall has an apse at the western end, and on the half-dome which roofs the apse, beneath which the Duke sat to grant audiences to his people, was painted a large cross. In the southern wing is a chapel which was obviously of great importance for it is one of the largest rooms in the palace, smaller only than the audience chamber and the great council chamber. In the chapel, between the twin columns that supported the vaulting, the excavators found a fine marble reliquary, shaped like a sarcophagus, but too small ever to have contained a body since it measures only some 33 in x 18 in and is about 27 in high. The lid was fastened with metal clamps, and has a central hole for the pouring in of libations. On the face of the reliquary is carved a cross, and on the lid is a cross-shaped recess with rivet holes, showing that a metal (perhaps a golden) cross was once attached. It must have contained the bones of a saint or some other valuable relic, but when found it had been broken open and emptied.

The daily purpose of this relic, in its central position in the palace chapel, was—as Richard Goodchild points out—almost certainly the administering of oaths. It was, in other words, an instrument of government, indispensable and in constant demand. Also, the libation hole suggests that from time to time it was the centre of some special ritual.

However limited were the resources of the Duke of Britain as compared with the Duke of Cyrenaica, his palace would have had the three essential features—audience chamber, council chamber and chapel. In the audience chamber, Arthur sat to give judgment, to hear complaints, to receive the kings and their legates, and to transact all the public business of his busy office. In the council chamber he sat with his commanders and staff, with Caius and Drustans, Wlanca and others, to make decisions about his campaigns, about the defence of the island,

and the government of Britain. In the chapel litigants would appear to take the oath, or allies would come to swear allegiance to Arthur's administration.

The Duke of Britain, like the Duke of Cyrenaica, would have had a reliquary upon which these oaths could be taken, as a necessary instrument of his administration. Indeed, such an object would be as usual and inevitable in an official building of this period as is a Bible in a modern police court.

If Joseph had indeed brought with him the dish reputedly used at the Last Supper, here was a relic—sanctified by long sojourn in Britain to Britain's especial worship—both appropriate and available. Joseph would have deposited it in his church of St Mary at Glastonbury. William of Malmesbury wrote that 'Men of that province had no oath more frequent or more sacred, than to swear by the Old Church, fearing the swiftest vengeance on their perjury in this respect.' Perhaps the special binding quality of the oath was due to the presence in that church of the sacred dish.

Arthur's name is linked closely with Glastonbury and we have seen that he paid special devotion to the Virgin Mary. Since Joseph's church at Glastonbury was dedicated to Mary, this too provides a link. Arthur might well have deposited the relic in his official residence, to be an instrument as well as a symbol of his authority over the Christian part of the island. If Joseph had not brought it the mere tradition of his having done so would of itself have had potency, and a physical symbol of the tradition would no doubt have been invented or found.

So the Holy Grail, either Joseph's or some symbolic substitute, would lie in Arthur's palace, worthily preserved in a gorgeous reliquary, inlaid with gold and studded with gems. The miraculous spear was kept with it. On special days the reliquary would be shown to the congregation, and carried in solemn procession, a blaze of candles illumining the chapel, the choir chanting and the incense rising to the roof. Sometimes, in the communion service, the transmuted bread was served to the selected communicants from what was, or was reputed to be, the very dish used by Christ. Such solemnity could well give rise to legend and leave its mark on the story. In time the relic would have come to symbolise Arthur's power and to have represented the Christian unity of Britain, overriding both the authority of the regional kings and the opposing forces which Arthur could barely hold in check.

Behind the story of the quest we can surmise the capture of the Grail by rebellious elements in Britain. By seizing this central instrument and token of Arthur's power, perhaps they hoped to undermine his authority and to re-establish the independence of their kingdoms. The discovery and achievement of the Grail by Arthur's followers would then have been of tremendous importance and its dominant place in the legends becomes comprehensible.

There is evidence to support belief in a theft of the Grail. The *Life of St Gildas* relates that Arthur at one stage besieged Glastonbury, to take Guenever who was there. For the Christian leader to be besieging the central shrine of Christianity in Britain is certainly odd, but if divisions were beginning to appear among Arthur's followers, the theft of the Grail could have ensued. We have already seen that Gildas ends his *Destruction of Britain* with an astonishing outburst against Mother Church who has rejected her true sons, pointing to divisions and schism in the Christian world. If one group had seized the Grail for political reasons, then dividing passions would have been aroused and the breach would have been deep and bitter.

This would explain the connection in the legends, otherwise so hard to understand, between the Holy Grail and the civil war in which Arthur was finally engulfed. The Grail, the symbol of good, is shown as the spring of evil and unhappy events. If it were the centre of a struggle for power, and a symbol of that power, the connection becomes explicable.

Although the Grail seems to have been recovered by Arthur's men, at some point thereafter it was irrevocably lost, to leave succeeding generations in doubt as to its very existence. Perhaps it was too valuable and too potent a relic to be allowed to remain an article of contention between the two parties. Perhaps one group, whose political ambition was greater than their piety, destroyed it lest it should fall into the hands of their rivals. So the Grail vanished, leaving only a fable, which nevertheless contains some glimpses of the truth and of the pomp and glory that once surrounded it—the pomp of candles and of gold, and the glory of faith.

XIII

ARTHUR'S BIRTH AND DEATH

TO find an approximate year for Arthur's birth, two
writers who link his name with that of Ambrosius must
be examined. First is William, the monk of Malmesbury,
who wrote his *Chronicle of the Kings of England* during the
first half of the twelfth century. He was chiefly concerned with
the story of the English people and not with the story of the
Britons; he relied, as he himself says, upon English sources such
as the *Anglo-Saxon Chronicle*; and his precise purpose was to
write a coherent account of the English kings. Nevertheless, as a
background to his main story, he sketches the campaigns of Constantine and of Maximus and gives a full account of Vortigern's
activities. He describes how the English came as allies of the
Britons, pretending that they would 'defend the Province in
the East, while they might curb the Scots on the northern
frontier.'

For these events he must have gone to British sources and not
merely to the English documents which he mentioned. And his
description of the first English as allies who turned upon the
Britons, rather than as raiding conquerors, is a statement of the
British point of view. That he was using a British source is further
indicated by his description of the first English as 'presumptuous
barbarians'. He records that he was induced to write his book
'out of love to my country', and he would not have spontane-
ously described his ancestors as 'presumptuous barbarians'. The

words are far more likely to have been written originally by a Briton, and to have been transcribed by William when copying the account of Ambrosius. In spite of his main preoccupation with events after the English conquest, we thus obtain from his work some account of the activities of the Britons drawn from British sources.

William of Malmesbury was a careful and scholarly writer, whose evidence should not be disregarded merely because he was writing 500 or 600 years after the main struggle between the English and the Britons. He would have drawn upon the best sources he could find, and have used them critically.

He writes of Ambrosius :

> When [Vortimer, son of Vortigern] died, the British strength decayed, and all hope fled from them; and they would soon have perished altogether had not Ambrosius, the sole survivor of the Romans who became monarch after Vortigern, quelled the presumptuous barbarians by the powerful aid of warlike Arthur.

The description of Ambrosius as the sole survivor of the Romans echoes, with a slight variation, the phrase of Gildas that Ambrosius was 'alone of his Roman family' by chance left alive. This passage of Gildas is itself ambiguous. It is only because he mentioned the death of the parents of Ambrosius that we know he is saying that Ambrosius was the sole survivor of his Roman *family* (which is credible), rather than that he was the sole survivor of the Roman *people* (which is not). William omits the reference to the parents of Ambrosius. He is unlikely to have done so if he had the full text of Gildas in front of him, for this is a significant and interesting detail.

This similarity of phrase, coupled with this difference, suggests that William of Malmesbury was making use of a source which contained some of the traditions of the Britons but was not Gildas's book. This is supported by the fact that Gildas makes no mention of Arthur in his chapter on Ambrosius, whereas William does. Moreover, William's source does not seem to have been the text of Nennius, whose chapter on Arthur makes no mention of Ambrosius. Therefore William must have had access to some British document which is now lost. The new fact he produces from this postulated source is that Arthur was fighting at the same time as Ambrosius, and was subordinate to him. Chronologically this is not impossible.

The entry of the *Annales Cambriae* giving the date of Arthur's death as 537, records that he died in battle; other traditions suggest that he died of wounds received in battle. In either case, at the time of his death he was obviously still capable of bearing arms. He could not have been very young, since he died some twenty years after the suggested date of Mount Badon, which was the climax of his career and presumably took place during his prime. It is reasonable to assume that Arthur was in his middle sixties at the time of his death, and that he was in his middle forties at the time of Badon. He would thus have been born in or about 472. His birth would have coincided approximately with the breakout of the English, and he would have spent his childhood and come to manhood in the days of the leadership of Ambrosius.

If, as shown earlier, Ambrosius died some time before 495, Arthur would then have been in his early twenties. He might well have served his apprenticeship with Ambrosius, and could have held a junior command under him. Later, when his own massive victories had been achieved, and when his dominating reputation had developed, his early association with Ambrosius was remembered with advantage: to Arthur, however junior his command at the time may have been, some of the successes of Ambrosius were later ascribed. He was remembered as having been magnificently victorious in his later wars with the English. If there were any record of his having served under Ambrosius, later writers would have assumed that it was with his skilful aid, and through the efforts of his golden youth, that the elderly Ambrosius had conquered.

There is some indication that William of Malmesbury tried to check from other sources the facts that he had transcribed, but found it impossible to do so. The very next sentence in his book sounds as if written after a vain search for further evidence.

It is of this Arthur that the Britons fondly tell so many fables, even to the present day; a man worthy to be celebrated, not by idle fictions, but by authentic history. He long upheld the sinking state, and roused the broken spirit of his countrymen to war.

The passage also suggests that William, in rejecting the main body of fable and tradition, was satisfied as to the authenticity of the few facts he gives.

There follows next his account of the Battle of Badon.

Finally, at the siege of Mount Badon, relying on an image of the Virgin, which he had affixed to his armour, he engaged nine hundred of the enemy, single handed, and dispersed them with incredible slaughter.

Again William is relying upon a source different from Nennius and one which he trusts. In the latter's account Arthur carries the image of the Virgin not at Badon, but at the Battle of Guinnion. Nennius, too, does not say that there were 900 English engaged but gives a similar figure (960) as the number of English casualties. This reaffirms approximately the numbers engaged at Badon as given by Nennius; it confirms that this was a victory which Arthur achieved without allies; and it confirms that Arthur had a special regard for the worship of the Virgin Mary—fresh and independent evidence of Arthur's specific devotion which is significant when we consider his traditional links with the church dedicated to her at Glastonbury.

This chronology, however, leads to one difficulty. Arthur would have been too young at the time of the death of Ambrosius to have succeeded forthwith to the full leadership of Britain and of the army. For a gap of a few years power would have been held by some older man. Just such a chain of events is described in Geoffrey of Monmouth's story of Uther Pendragon. According to Geoffrey, Ambrosius was poisoned as a result of a plot between the Saxons and Vortigern's surviving son, Pascentius. He was succeeded by his brother Uther Pendragon. (Uther's second name was derived from the dragon wrought in gold which he took as his standard. This sounds authentic enough as the dragon was the heraldic symbol of the Britons.)

Geoffrey also writes of Uther Pendragon's war with Octha, the son of Hengist, whom he slew in battle near St Albans. Uther Pendragon himself died in the same city shortly after. He too was poisoned; and we may suspect Geoffrey of inventing this for it follows too closely the tale he tells of Ambrosius. However, if Geoffrey is here partly recording a true tradition, this does give an approximate date for the death of Uther Pendragon. For the *Anglo-Saxon Chronicle* says that in 488 Hengist's son succeeded to the kingdom and was king of the men of Kent twenty-four winters. Uther Pendragon and Octha, according to Geoffrey, died in the same year. This gives 512 as the year of Arthur's succession or election to the leadership of Britain. He would have been about forty at the time, and some of his twelve battles may already have been fought. It is significant that Nennius introduces his chapter on Arthur with the words

> When Hengist was dead, Octha his son crossed from the left hand side of Britain into the kingdom of the Cantii, and from him are descended the kings of the Cantii. Then Arthur fought against those people in those days.

Again there is a link between Arthur's command and the events of Octha's life.

Geoffrey also makes Arthur the son of Uther Pendragon by the wife of the Duke of Cornwall. The detailed circumstances surrounding this story are fanciful. Uther by magical arts takes on the likeness of the Duke of Cornwall, and so gains the bed of Igerna, the Duke's wife, and Arthur is conceived. The story cannot be factual and Arthur's birth during the leadership of Uther Pendragon must be rejected. All that we are entitled to conclude from it is that the reference by Gildas to the progeny of Ambrosius may well refer to Arthur.

We now have a framework of dates within which to fit Arthur's life. Though the evidence is shadowy and much has to be assumed and inferred, the results do not contradict any of the statements of the sources. It is true that parts of Geoffrey's testimony have been rejected and other parts accepted; but the nature of his book makes this the only course. For the rest, the tentative dates fit the few firm facts, and a feasible chronology emerges.

Arthur's tragic death marked the end of effective resistance by the Britons. Thenceforward the English were able swiftly to occupy almost the whole of the diocese; the dream vanished of driving them back into the sea, or even of containing them in the south-eastern corner of the island. Only in the mountainous regions of Wales did the Britons bring the English to a halt; there the struggle continued for a further 700 years. The title of Prince of Wales is a memorial to the invincibility of the Britons in their last corner of the island, and to the recognition by the English kings that total conquest of the Roman diocese was impossible. But with Arthur's passing, Roman Britain finally passed, and the final foundation of England began. Within a few years the English felt themselves sufficiently secure to cease calling reinforcements from their German homeland. Nennius says that these landings ended in the reign of Ida; and Ida began to reign in 547, only ten years after Arthur's death. The English indeed now saw the whole island as theirs, and looked upon further immigrants (even of their own race) as raiders and invaders.

Arthur's death sharply divides the two stories of Britain and of England; and it marked the end of all real hope for the Britons. It is small wonder that his death became the heart of his story. Its sadness was made more bitter by the knowledge that he was killed not by the invading English, but by rebel Britons, in ungrateful and suicidal revolt against his authority. His own kinsman, Mordred, led the battle against him. Both the historical importance and the woeful irony of the event made it the central point and tragic climax of the legends. The death of

Arthur, the *Morte d'Arthur*, was the title and theme of Malory's great collection of legend. The despair in which it left the Britons made them reluctant to believe that they had irrevocably lost him, and with him their last hope of success. Stories circulated that he had not died, but had gone to be healed of his wounds. He would return with his companions, and would once more lead the army of Britain to victory. These rumours were probably believed immediately after his death, because without this belief there was no hope. But later a fabulous element was added to the stories to defeat the logic of time. Arthur was waiting, immortal with his old companions, and would ride again to Britain's rescue when need arose. He became the king that had been and was to be. Not only his memory but he himself was deathless, and he would come again when Britain was in peril. There were older stories of other immortals; and it was but natural that unwilling belief in Arthur's loss should have merged with these and joined Arthur's name to them.

One fact is clear. These tales could not have come to birth if Arthur had died before his followers' eyes in battle, nor if he had been publicly and solemnly buried in a known and noted grave. He cannot have been slain outright in his last fight; he must have died of his wound afterwards, in some quiet retreat. The *Black Book of Carmarthen* contains a verse dealing with the graves of famous men.

> A grave for March, a grave for Gwythur; a grave for Gwgawn of the red sword; not wise (the thought) a grave for Arthur.

Thus Arthur's grave was unknown, and so notoriously that the fact had become proverbial. True, at Glastonbury his tomb was said to have been discovered, with a coffin bearing his name, and the epitaph *King that was, and King that shall be*. But this claim is not generally accepted.

Although the place of Arthur's burial is lost, the time and place of his last battle are known. In the *Annales Cambriae*, under the date 537, is the entry 'The battle of Camlann, in which

Arthur and Medraut perished and there was a plague in Britain and in Ireland.' Although the words are otherwise Latin, the name of the battle is written in the old tongue of the Britons: *Gueith cam lann*, the Battle of Camlann. This suggests that the entry is taken from an older record, written in the language of the men who took part in the events, and likely be to be authentic.

Where was Camlann?

In an article in *Antiquity* in 1935 (No. IX, p. 289), O. G. S. Crawford suggests that Camlann was the old Roman fort of Camboglanna on the Wall. This place (the modern Birdoswald) lies on the western stretch of Hadrian's great frontier work. North of it lie the thickly wooded Scottish lowlands where Arthur had earlier fought the Battle of Celidon. The area was far from the English invaders, and this last battle must have been a resumption of the war which Arthur had waged against the Britons of the North West who resented his leadership. More than twenty years earlier he had marched this way, and on his return from victory beyond the Wall had fought a further battle at Chester. Now, twenty years after Badon, the North West was again in revolt against him, and on this occasion there was a vital and tragic difference. Not only the local kings and chieftains were seeking to pull him down; some of his own companions, their work against the Saxons over, had joined his enemies.

One tradition (which Malory uses and expands) says that Arthur's own son and nephew, Mordred, was leader of the revolt, and was seeking to seize power from Arthur. Mordred is evidently the Medraut of the *Annales Cambriae*, and Malory thus seems to be recording an accurate tradition. If, as our scheme of dates suggests, Arthur was now in his sixties, it is not impossible that a younger rival was beginning to emerge. Men would begin to ask who should take his place as commander of all the forces of Britain, and claimants to the succession would begin to appear. Arthur had been the third member of his family to hold this command, having succeeded Ambrosius and Uther, so that a kinsman would have had a powerful claim. Nor is it impossible that an ambitious and impatient claimant should make common cause with Arthur's former enemies, even with those who considered that a general commander represented a threat to their regional independence, and who had sought to destroy both Arthur and his command. Such paradoxical alliances are not uncommon. Mordred, Arthur's nephew or kinsman, could have promised the discontented kings that he would be their servant not their master, and that in his hands the supreme office would no longer be a threat to their independence or to their sovereignty.

Although the *Annales Cambriae* do not say that Arthur and Mordred were opponents, merely that both perished in the same battle, they clearly support the legend of Mordred's revolt. As both Malory and Geoffrey of Monmouth recount it, Arthur was away on the Continent when Mordred made his final attempt to seize power. The old fellowship was split, and the companions of Arthur divided.

Frequently in his book Malory seems to be giving historical facts, and his description of Mordred's revolt against Arthur reads as such. He says (in Book XXI) that Mordred 'araised much people about London, for they of Kent, Southsex, and Surrey, Estsex, and of Southfolk and of Northfolk, held the most part with Sir Mordred.' This list of counties, or rather of Saxon kingdoms, is an accurate list of the areas which by this date were firmly in English hands. Here perhaps an accurate tradition is preserved, recording that Mordred, to defeat Arthur, made common cause with the English. Until this happened, the English and Arthur's Britons seem to have been uneasily at peace. The *Anglo-Saxon Chronicle* mentions no battle between them after the capture of the Isle of Wight, in 530, until 552. A peace of some kind had clearly been made.

Perhaps while Arthur, feeling secure against the English, was quelling revolts in the North, Mordred and his Saxon allies marched to support the rebels there. Arthur, ageing but still formidable, gathered his army together for the last time and took the road to the Wall to forestall the meeting of his enemies. He arrived too late, to find Mordred with his southern army already organising the North against him. On hearing of his coming Mordred and his allies took refuge in the old fort of Camboglanna.

After the raids of the barbarians in 375, the fort had never been reoccupied; but the buildings would for the most part have been standing, and the walls and ramparts firm. Seeing some of the Roman fortifications that survive today, 1,600 years and more after their building, the deserted fort as Mordred saw it, a mere 160 years after its earlier occupation, can well be imagined. Silent and dusty, the barracks and dark store rooms unswept, with drifting leaf mould settling upon the floors, the rampart overgrown, it was still a formidable and almost impregnable place. The army of Mordred which, according to Geoffrey of Monmouth, was a general coalition of all the opponents of Arthur— Saxons, Picts and Scots joined with the dissident Britons—might have felt fairly safe behind its walls.

When Arthur's forces appeared there was, according to Malory, a period of negotiation and parley. Considering the nature of the battle and the fact that on either side were old friends and former companions, this sounds likely. Perhaps there was talk of Arthur's peacefully laying down his command to make way for a young man. But whatever the nature of the parley, the truce was broken. In the ensuing battle Mordred fell, slain by Arthur's own hand, and Arthur himself received wounds from which he later died. His army had been broken, and most of his companions scattered. There remained with him Bedevere, who helped him from the battlefield. He was taken by boat to be healed of his wounds. One version of the legend takes him back to Glastonbury, where he is said to have been buried, but it is a time of confusion with no clear order or government left in Britain, and in the confusion Arthur vanishes.

Before he died, deserted by all but a few, his army shattered and the work of twenty-five years laid in ruin, Arthur may have pondered, in the loneliness of defeat and the pain of his mortal wounds, why he had failed, and what causes had brought him from the triumph of Badon to the sorrow of Camlann. Military genius and military leadership had not been enough. He had seen Britain as a province to be defended, and her mixed people as potential soldiers in his cause. But he had failed to give to those people, or to their separate kings, any permanent understanding of his methods. The unity he had insisted upon, at the sword's edge when necessary, had been a purely military unity, devised for the sole purpose of defeating the English, and when that purpose had been achieved at Badon, he had no motives to offer for a continuance of his policies. He had been a commander, not a leader; a soldier, not a king. True, he had invoked the Christian cause, but this had seemed but an instrument with which to fashion the single command that he needed.

Arthur could have had no foreknowledge of his fame or of the enduring quality of his success. For twenty years the old people of Britain and the new English folk had shared the island. There was hostility between them but there was also respect. After the victories of Arthur, neither could ever despise the other. Thus to the ultimate unity of the island, which he had been unable to maintain in his lifetime, Arthur had permanently contributed.

At the time it seemed that Britain had destroyed herself irrevocably. The army of Britain would never be re-formed. The last echo of Rome died away in the silence after the battle, and from now on the new English people would swiftly conquer almost the entire province. The centrifugal forces would tear Britain apart, making her an easy prey for the invaders. Camlann was the beginning of a longer and ultimately fatal civil war. Henceforth the Britons were to turn their swords against one another, with kings and chieftains striving for illusory sovereignty in kingdoms of which they were to be totally deprived.

With the army of Britain destroyed, the English no longer had to limit their activities to the South East. Within ten years of Camlann, in 547, new landings were made in the North. Ida, predecessor of the kings of Northumbria, sailed from Germany, and there is archaeological evidence that landings were made on the Tyne estuary at the eastern end of the Wall. From there the English marched westwards along the old frontier. There is evidence too that by a crowning irony they stopped at Camboglanna. Maybe they saw, round about the fort, traces of the old battle where their great adversary had taken his death wound, and where their inheritance of the island had been made possible.

XIV

ARTHUR OF BRITAIN

O UR quest has been long, leading to Caesar and to
Claudius; to the hero Caractacus, and to the ambitions
and folly of Albinus who first led away the legions from
Britain; to Britain's first experiment as an independent power
under Carausius, and to her triumphs on the Continent under
Constantine and Maximus; to the days when the Angles and
Saxons first landed as Treaty Troops in the South East, and to
the time of their rebellion and break-out into the island as a
whole. We have seen the vain appeal of the Council of Britain
to Rome, and the stubborn way in which Britain defended herself.

Not only in time have we travelled, but across many lands:
we have seen the invasion armies of Rome embarking in Gaul;
the Scots coming from Ireland, and the tough and warlike Picts
marching southwards from Caledonia. We have seen the fair-
haired Frisian and German sailors landing at Lympne and Dover,
and their cousins the Alemanni settling as garrison troops under
their leader Fraomar. The armies of Britain, though Britain herself was beset, have sailed to Gaul and marched along the dusty
roads to Spain and Italy and to Rome itself. We have seen them
defeated at Aquiliea and living out their lives in exile in Armorica,
naming the province of Brittany after their homeland as some
comfort to them when they remembered the former triumphs
of their arms.

ARTHUR'S ———
——— BRITAIN

CALEDONIA

HADRIAN'S WALL

CAMLANN
Camboglanna

YORK
Eboracum

Camulodonum

River Trent

LINCOLN
Lindum Colonia

THE WASH

BOURNE
River Glen

BRANCASTER
Branodunum

CHESTER
Deva

BURGH CASTLE
Gariannonum

ANGLES

WALTON CASTLE

GLOUCESTER
Glevum

St. ALBANS
Verulanium

BRADWELL
Othona

RECULVER
Regulbium

CIRENCESTER
Corinium

SILCHESTER
Calleva

BAYDON

LONDON
Londinium

SAXONS

RICHBOROUGH
Rutupiae

KINGDOM OF AMBROSIUS

GLASTONBURY

WINCHESTER

DOVER
Dubris

LYMPNE
Lemanis

PORCHESTER
Portus Adurni

PEVENSEY
Anderida

EXETER
Isca

CHICHESTER
Noviomagus

ISLE OF
WIGHT

At the end of the quest Arthur ceases to be a merely legendary personage and becomes a credible and real figure. The inventions of Geoffrey of Monmouth and of Malory are seen as mere additions to a story which basically is true. The silence of Gildas and the tantalising brevity of Nennius alike contribute to the final picture.

The picture that emerges is not that of Arthur of Cornwall, nor Arthur of Strathclyde, nor Arthur the petty king of some mountain region. Nor is it Arthur the bandit, nor Arthur the half-forgotten commander of a local levy. It is the picture of Arthur of Britain, of a man who imposed unity on a group of separate kingdoms, who maintained the concept that the island of Britain, from the Wall to the Channel, was one country, and who bequeathed this concept to his enemies the English.

Indeed, were there no written evidence of his existence, the course of history would compel us to assume that such a leader lived and fought and, at least for a time, was victorious. Although Maximus had stripped the island of all the Roman troops, and Continental writers (Procopius and Prosper Tiro) were saying as early as AD 441 that the provinces of Britain were reduced to subjection by the Saxons, the *Anglo-Saxon Chronicle* makes it clear that the English were compelled to fight for almost every yard of ground. The Saxons landed at some date close to AD 447, yet it is not until about 120 years later, in 571, that the *Chronicle* tells of a battle as far east as Bedford, and of the capture of Lenbury, Aylesbury, Benson and Ensham. The Britons were a stubborn and warlike nation, and had obviously found leaders able and courageous enough to give the Saxons pause.

Now that the evidence has been examined, we can summarise the narrative. Arthur was born in AD 473 or thereabouts, at the time when the English first broke out of Kent where they had been settled. He grew up under Ambrosius and, as a young man, saw what leadership and organisation could achieve. Although Britain was now divided into many kingdoms, the memory of central rule was strong, and men flocked to Ambrosius from the whole island. Ambrosius died when Arthur was about twenty and Uther Pendragon, more a Briton than a Roman, taking the national emblem of the dragon as his standard, became commander. He too was successful in resisting the English. When he died, there was some doubt about the succession to the central command. A man named Caius may have had some claim to the office, but Arthur, a kinsman of Ambrosius, and therefore a member of the royal house of Damnonia, defeated a Saxon army and returned triumphantly with the sword of his enemy as a trophy, making his own claim irresistible.

Immediately on his appointment, which took place around 512 (the date of Uther's death), Arthur promoted Caius to be his deputy, and appointed other officers of his own choosing.

He discarded the dragon standard of Uther and, adopting Christian ensigns, made it clear that he wished to lead all the Christian inhabitants of the island, whether they were of British descent or not. He had to consider the descendants of the Germanic settlers like the Alemanni who had come under their King Fraomar, perhaps converts among some of the Saxons, and the ex-legionaries and their descendants from all the provinces of the Empire. For this mixed population the dragon standard of the Britons had little meaning. By bearing the Cross of Christ and the image of the Virgin Mary, Arthur made clear that he was fighting for all, and that he desired and deserved the loyalties of each one of them.

He was granted, or he assumed, the title of Duke of Britain and set about giving real substance to the office. With the exception of the posts on the Wall which had come to an end in the days of Maximus and which there was little hope of re-establishing, Arthur appointed men to command all the garrisons and forts which former Dukes of Britain had possessed, and formed them into a council. At first he did not appoint governors for the two provinces of Maxima Caesariensis and Valentia, for these had to be of consular rank and he still had hopes of making contact with Rome, the source of all legal power. However, when this hope faded, he appointed a nephew to one of these provinces.

With armies drawn from all the kingdoms of Britain, with the adventurers who had come to him from the Continent and with the aid of his council of commanders, he fought successfully against the Saxons, defeating them on many occasions. His chief adversary was the Cerdic of the *Anglo-Saxon Chronicle*, who had come to Britain in 495. Cerdic was not a Saxon, being probably of British descent settled somewhere on the river Loire. But he had thrown in his lot with the Saxons and became one of their greatest leaders.

As Duke of Britain, Arthur obtained from Glastonbury for his official headquarters a holy relic, the dish reputed to have been used by Christ at the Last Supper and brought to Britain by Joseph of Arimathea. The dish, housed in a magnificent reliquary, was a basic tool of daily administration, and was sometimes taken in solemn and splendid procession; on special occasions it was used in the communion service attended by his council of commanders. The church at Glastonbury, said to have been built by Joseph, was dedicated to the Virgin Mary and Arthur emphasised his devotion to this centre of British Christianity by using the image of Mary as one of his standards.

Because his was the Christian cause rather than merely the British cause, Arthur went to the aid of Saxon or Germanic people who had settled in Britain and become Christian. One was Leode-Grance, with whom he allied himself, and whose daughter Winifred he married.

To begin with, his battles had as their aim the securing of the existing frontiers between the land held by the English and the rest of the island. He was also concerned to defend the centres where arms were manufactured, since Continental supplies were no longer available. He was so successful in this that he brought about a period of peace when the commanders of the Saxon forts in the South East were numbered among his council, and British supremacy appeared assured.

The uneasy peace was broken, however. Some of the Britons were suspicious of Arthur's willingness to support men of other races, and suspicious of his alien wife. Reluctantly, but recognising the political necessity, Arthur sent his wife back to her own people. As escort he sent Wlanca, a soldier of Germanic blood, who had come over to fight in Arthur's army after the Frankish invasion of his own territory of Burgundy.

The war was resumed and culminated in the overwhelming defeat of the English in 517 at Mount Badon. Arthur's military policy had proved triumphant. The English seemed firmly and permanently confined to their parts of the island. Elsewhere the life of Britain was resumed and the province prospered. Freed from the threat of the English, men turned to the almost forgotten occupations of peace. The Church flourished, with gratitude for the great deliverance an added spur to worship. The framework of government which Arthur had established for warlike purposes continued to hold the nation together. Magistrates administered justice and public men and private citizens discharged their duties with enthusiasm and loyalty. It seemed that the golden age had returned, with law and justice firmly established.

But the centrifugal forces, the regional loyalties and local ambitions which Arthur had curbed, were soon to be reawakened. The generation grew old that remembered the terrors from which Arthur had saved them. As they died, so the memory of Badon and of the miracle that Arthur had brought about began to be forgotten. Many of the kings, particularly those in the North who had never fully accepted him, saw no reason why Arthur's office should continue. They felt safe to resume their regional monarchies, without the curb of a central military leader.

Arthur was by now a comparatively old man and one of his kinsmen, Mordred, saw himself as successor. He made secret promises to the kings and assured them that if they supported him for the office, he would exercise it very differently from Arthur, as their servant and protector, not their ruler.

Arthur's enemies among his own people conspired to remove

the sacred dish from his chapel. This relic, upon which oaths had been taken by Arthur's allies, by men coming to him with claims and suits, and by his defeated enemies, had become a symbol of his authority. Many of his officers attempted its recovery and it was Galerius Hadrianus, son of Wlanca, who succeeded. Once again the relic was placed in Arthur's chapel and used in the communion service. Galerius Hadrianus, who had been appointed governor of the second of the consular provinces, died shortly afterwards. The relic was stolen a second time and finally disappeared.

Meantime, Arthur's council of commanders was sadly reduced in size, for some had died and many had gone over to Mordred's party. Arthur had now to face a new and more bitter struggle. Never again, after their defeat at Badon, would a Saxon army stand against him in the field. But now the Christian part of the island was itself divided, and Arthur had to fight new enemies from among his old companions. The theft of the relic had split the Christian population of the island in two. Monks famous for their piety railed against the Church, and soldiers who had followed Arthur's Christian banner now took the field against him. This struggle kindled the old half-hidden conflict between Arthur and the kings of Britain, who had followed him when there was danger, but who feared and resented him now that he had won them safety.

Also the Picts in the North were still hostile. Arthur was forced once more to buckle on his armour, and to take the field against his northern foes. Perhaps it was then that he captured and executed Hueil, the brother of Gildas. Worse was to follow. Some of the impatient kings raised the North, which had been hostile to Arthur from the beginning. Remote from the dangers of the English, the kings of those regions in particular could see little purpose in supporting a too-dominant Duke of Britain; with the Saxons defeated they were glad to settle old scores with him.

Mordred, together with those of the Companions who supported him, marched North to join them. Arthur, now in his sixties, weakened by the years and embittered by the ingratitude and enmity of those whose battles he had fought, marched to do battle. The two armies met at Camlann on the Wall, and there in 537 Arthur received his death wound.

A few faithful followers took him south to die. The discipline and order which he had imposed upon his men operated even in defeat. The arms of his defeated army, together with his own sword and armour, were gathered up and returned for repair to the place where they had been made. This was the habit of discipline only, for the battle was not to be renewed, nor the cause repaired.

So died Arthur of Britain who for twenty years and more had been the bastion of Christian Britain against the heathen English; who had defeated the English, only to be defeated in his turn by rebellion, schism and civil war; who lived long enough to know the bitterness of defeat and whose death meant the end of all hope for the Britons. After Camlann, even those who had plotted against him knew that his death was a tragedy, and that the Roman Island had reached the end of her story. Henceforth, followers and enemies alike remembered the death of Arthur as a great and sorrowful event marking the end of a nation's history, and the passing away of the old land of Britain.

But Arthur, Duke of Britain, had not lived in vain nor had his success been as ephemeral as must have appeared immediately after his death. Although the divisions among his followers seemed tragically to have undone the work of Badon and all the labour of the preceding years, that work in fact has endured in part to this day.

During a period of twenty or thirty years, from the late 490s to 517, Arthur had defeated the English in a series of campaigns and his administration and army had continued to deny any swift or wholesale victory to the invading English. The latter had been compelled to live within limited areas of the island as neighbours, albeit hostile, of the Britons and the old mixed population. The first generation of mutinous Treaty Troops and of the piratical adventurers who came as reinforcements died out, and Arthur's resistance gave time for a new generation of the English to come to maturity. These were men who had been born in the island, who had seen more of it than bloodstained invasion beaches and the heavy smoke of burned villas and sacked towns. They had grown up on their fathers' farms in Kent or Sussex and had learned something of the history of the province, and of the brave men who dwelt there. There had been time, between the fighting, for folk of the two nations to intermarry, and for some Saxons to serve with the Britons and some Britons with the Saxons.

Had the first English swiftly swept away all British resistance, the history of the new country would have been very different. The English would not have inherited a sense of political unity of their new land. The separate kingdoms which they set up would have continued separate for many more generations, as happened in other provinces of the Empire. Bede tells us that as early as the latter part of the fifth century Aelle, King of the South Saxons, exercised authority over all the English south of the Humber, and in the latter half of the sixth century Cealwin of the West Saxons exercised the same power. Thenceforward this authority was held regularly by various of the English kings who took the title of *Bretwalda* or Lord of Britain, demonstrating that they recognised the unity of the old Roman province as overriding the separate kingdoms. The example of Arthur had thus endured, hastening the foundation of the kingdom of England. The time he gained, indeed, ensured that the kingdom of England should come to being and that, alone of the former provinces of the Empire, Britain did not remain until later times a patchwork of separate and independent territories. The English had seen, and had felt to their hurt, the power of a Duke of Britain acting as leader of the wars and organising the armies of the individual kings. Under the new title of *Bretwalda* they soon established such a central authority themselves. It was the struggle for this office that finally unified the several English kingdoms. The kings of England are the heirs of the *Bretwaldas*, and through them of Arthur.

The time that Arthur won on the River Glen and at Mount Badon preserved for posterity not only the concept of a unified Britain, which has come down to us as the concept of a unified England. It ensured that the old mixed population was neither totally destroyed nor wholly expelled, and so brought into being a new nation, neither wholly Germanic nor wholly Romanised Celtic, but a unique mixture of both. The fifth man to hold the office of *Bretwalda*, Edwin of Northumbria, reigned (according to Bede) over both Englishmen and Britons. Arthur had prevented the total destruction of the Britons and the two nations were learning to live side by side, first as enemies, then as subjects of a single Lord of Britain. If today the divisions of these peoples are blurred, and the individual folk no longer to be seen (save in Wales) as separate groups, this is not because his labours have been frustrated. On the contrary, the custom of living together overwhelmed the separate identities of the groups, and all have merged into the single identity of the English people.

Thanks to Arthur, and to others whose names are forgotten, the English conquest was far from being one of complete annihilation. The blood of the tribes of Britain, of the Brigantes, the Atrebates, the Iceni and others, flows in the veins of Englishmen today, and the character of England contains much of the character of Britain. Through the long war and uneasy peace the two nations learned and copied from one another. When, 500 years after Arthur, the Household Troops of Harold died axe in hand at Hastings, even though further fight was useless and retreat would have been honourable, the methods of the first English were clearly evident. But when Hereward took to the Fens, and when generations earlier Alfred had retreated to Athelney the better to fight the Danes, it is not altogether fanciful to imagine that the English had learned something from the Britons, and that the armies of Alfred and Hereward owed a little to the traditions, character and blood of Caractacus.

Arthur's memorial is the mixed people of England, living in a kingdom, from the Wall to the Channel, that is still essentially the same area as that of the Roman province whose integrity he preserved and whose unity he projected into the future. The time he won for the Britons, and the delays he imposed upon the English, made possible the fusion of the two folk. The result is a people who speak a Germanic language but have a Celtic sense of poetry; they can fight in the manner of the first English, dying where they stand when need is, and gaining strength from disaster, or they can hide in the hills and jungles of the world as did their forefathers the Britons; they are as unlike their cousins in Germany as they are unlike their purely Celtic neighbours.

The work of Badon endures and the unity which Arthur, Duke of Britain and last champion of the Roman cause, imposed upon the island, survived the defeat of Camlann. It became a preciou: legacy that he left to his enemies and, modified by time and the coming of other peoples, it lives on to this day.

APPENDICES

1: NOTE ON THE INSIGNIA OF THE DUKE OF BRITAIN

The Roman government maintained a complete list of official posts, both civil and military, throughout the Empire. This list, entitled the *Notitia Dignitatum* (see Chapter X) also gave the insignia of each of the high officers.

None of these lists survives in original, but there are four copies dating from the fifteenth and sixteenth centuries, which were made from an earlier copy formerly kept at Spires Cathedral. The original as well as the Spires Manuscript are now lost.

The four surviving copies give the text accurately but contain extremely inaccurate versions of the insignia. The armour, forts, and dresses featured in the badges have all been forced into fifteenth or sixteenth-century patterns. One of the copies was made in 1542 for Otho Henry, Count Palatine. He is said to have rejected the pictures and demanded more exact copies. I have therefore examined these second versions which are bound with the 1542 manuscript at the Bayerische Staatsbibliothek in Munich (reference Clm 10 291). The forts are of grey stone with red roofs, and seem much closer to Roman design. They thus appear to be more accurate copies of the lost Roman original. I am supported in this view by a mosaic in the British Museum (No. 57D) which comes from Carthage and is dated to about AD 500. This shows a fortified city in a manner very similar to that of the second version of the Munich copy. The illustration on page 8 (reproduced by kind permission of the librarian of the Bayerische Staatsbibliothek) shows the insignia of the Duke of Britain according to this second set of drawings in Otho Henry's

195

manuscript. So far as I am aware this has not previously been published.

If Arthur was indeed Duke of Britain, this design or some version of it would have been the insignia of his office.

B.S.

2: NOTE ON SOME ARTHURIAN SITES IN BRITAIN

A RTHUR'S memory is preserved not only in the pages of the chroniclers and story-tellers. His name haunts many places throughout Britain. Whether these topographical associations represent genuine continuing traditions going back to some original historic truth, it is difficult to say; a large number seem to have merely literary origins. Many of the local stories may owe their existence to Geoffrey of Monmouth and Malory, and to others who first recorded a link (often mistaken) between the places and the name of Arthur.

One of the best known of these places is GLASTONBURY. As seen in Chapter II, here an association is attested early, Arthur's name having been joined with that of Glastonbury by the author of *The Life of Gildas*.

Equally famous is the castle of TINTAGEL in Cornwall. But in this case there is no written reference earlier than that of Geoffrey of Monmouth. The French *High History of the Holy Graal* (written in the thirteenth century) also mentions the castle as being the place where Uther Pendragon, assuming by magical arts the likeness of King Gorlois, lay with the latter's wife and begot Arthur. Malory has a similar tale and describes Tintagel in some detail; in his version Gorlois is duke, not king. The castle is also said to be the burial place of Tristan and Iseult. But the present castle, which is Norman and later, cannot possibly have been seen by Arthur. However the geographical position of Tintagel is in favour of an Arthurian association, for it almost certainly lies in the western kingdom of Ambrosius, Arthur's great predecessor and commander.

Also in Cornwall is DOZMARY POOL, a lake about a mile

in circumference, lying between two hills—Row Tor and Rame Head. It is said to be the lake into which Bedivere threw Excalibur after Arthur's last battle. It has been suggested that this tale grew in modern times, after Tennyson had made the Bedivere story familiar. Crawford's identification (see Chapter XIII) of Arthur's last battlefield of Camlann with Camboglanna on Hadrian's Wall makes the link between Dozmary Pool and Sir Bedivere impossible to accept.

CAMELFORD, near Dozmary Pool, is said to be the site of the battle of Camlann. This tradition rests on Geoffrey of Monmouth's statement that the battle was fought 'on the river Cambula in Cornwall'. Geoffrey's 'Cambula' was taken to be the river Camel. But again Crawford's identification of the battlefield shows that while Geoffrey was reporting an almost correct place name, he was wrong to place the battle in Cornwall, and Camelford's claim must fail.

CADBURY CASTLE in Somerset has for centuries been identified as Arthur's Camelot. Leland in the sixteenth century writes as if there were no doubt whatever, adducing as evidence the many Roman coins turned up by the plough and the name of 'divers villages thereabout (that) bear the name of Camalet and other'. Camden, also writing in the 1500s, makes the identification with equal certainty. Later writers and map-makers—Stow, Speed, Musgrave and Stukely—concur. Recent archaeological investigation shows sixth-century occupation of the site by a group rich enough to import costly luxuries from abroad. However, we would expect this on a site so far to the west, Arthur or no Arthur. The beliefs of Leland and the others may have their origin in the mistaken association between Geoffrey's 'Cambula' and the various villages named Camel. While the place is undoubtedly an important sixth-century site, it may thus have no direct connection with Arthur. But it remains one of the most interesting and intriguing of the places linked with Arthur's name.

Welsh legend and poetry abound in references to Arthur. This is natural since the descendants of his own people, the Britons, survived there unconquered for many centuries. But there is no historical reason to believe that he or his followers were ever active there; again it is probably due to Geoffrey of Monmouth that many places in Wales have become associated with him. Of these, CAERLEON-UPON-USK is perhaps the best known. Geoffrey records that Arthur kept the feast of Pentecost there, and this is the first written record of any link with Arthur. The beauty of the meadows and groves, writes Geoffrey, and the magnificence of the royal palaces with lofty gilded roofs that adorned the city made it even rival the grandeur of Rome. He makes Caerleon one of the chief of Arthur's cities and records that Queen Guinever retired to a nunnery there. Caxton, in his preface to Malory's work, reinforced the association, for he refers to Camelot as being in Wales and describes the ruins of a city that can still be seen. He seems to be referring to Caerleon. But the statement of Caxton is contradicted by Malory himself who places Camelot at Winchester. Finally, the ninth battle of Arthur, described by Nennius as having been fought at the City of the Legions has been ascribed to Caerleon. But this too is probably based on a misunderstanding, and the battle is better placed at Chester. Caerleon's claim seems to rest upon the mistakes of Geoffrey and others, rather than upon any continuing traditions.

There are several isolated landmarks in Wales named after Arthur. About five miles south of Brecon are two mountain peaks known as 'ARTHUR'S CHAIR'. Here, it is said, he called together his followers and told them of his plan to found the fellowship of the Round Table. In the same county of Brecknockshire is a range of hills called 'GWELY ARTHUR', or Arthur's Bed. Almost certainly these sites have no connection with the Arthur of history. The names are folk-names, given long after his time to commemorate one who had become a national hero. PEN ARTHUR and COITEN ARTHUR (Arthur's Quoit, a huge rock in the bed of the river Swadde), both in Brecknockshire, no doubt were named in a similar way.

We can conceive the way these names came to Wales by imagining what would have happened if Britain had been finally and irrevocably destroyed in 1940. If refugees from the disaster had fled to join their kin in Canada, then generations hence a Mount Churchill might well be found in the Selkirk mountains, or a Winston's Seat in the Mackenzie range in North America.

The West Country and Wales are of course the areas where Arthur's people largely survived and where just possibly some tenuous threads of genuine tradition might have been found in topographical associations. But what of the country further east and in the North of England which was overrun by his enemies? Even here, there are many places associated with him.

WINCHESTER was said by Malory to have been Arthur's Camelot. Malory may have written this simply because Winchester had been a capital city in ancient days and therefore seemed an appropriate capital for Arthur's Britain. When Malory's book came to be printed, Caxton wrote that the Table Round might be seen at Winchester : the object said to be the Round Table was exhibited at Winchester Castle, and was widely accepted as genuine.

> And so great Arthur's seat ould Winchester prefers,
> Whose ould round table yet she vaunteth to be hers.

It is still there, but is now known to be modern. There is no reason to accept Malory's identification, nor the secondary stories that have sprung from it. In the same way, Caxton advanced the claim of DOVER, stating that Sir Gawaine's skull and Cradock's skull could be seen there. This again cannot be accepted.

In the North, CARLISLE is mentioned in many of the ballads about King Arthur :

> King Arthur lives in merry Carlisle
> And seemly is to see;
> And there with him Queene Guenever
> That bride so bright of blee.

Chrétien de Troyes in 'Le Chevalier au Lion' places King Arthur's Court at 'Carduel', but says that this is in Wales. The Northern ballad makers writing of King Arthur seem to have had no reasons other than local patriotism for associating him with Carlisle.

Scotland too claims many associations with Arthur. Near Liddesdale is a hill called ARTHUR'S SEAT. As this area has also been identified as the site of the Battle of Arderyad, mentioned by the *Annales Cambriae* as having been fought in about 573, it may be that the name is an echo of that conflict. More famous is Arthur's Seat in EDINBURGH. We know from a poem by the Scots writer Kennedy that this hill already bore the name in the late 1400s. Malory's King Lot of Lothian and Orkney has been taken to be Llew or Lothus, King of Lothian, whose traditional burial place is at Trapender. He is said to be Mordred's father, so that this area may well be Arthurian country. Moreover, Sir Gawaine's 'kin or well-willers to his brethren' are said by Malory to have been knights of Scotland.

But in general these local associations throughout the island have to be treated with great reserve. Often, as we have seen, they are comparatively recent—dating only from the days of Geoffrey or Malory, whose writings revived Arthur's fame as a national hero.

3: BIBLIOGRAPHICAL NOTE

ANNALES CAMBRIAE. A short Welsh chronicle covering the years 453 to 954. There are then twenty-three blank years, ending at 977, after which entries are resumed. It was written down in the late eleventh or early twelfth century, but copied from an older manuscript. It can be taken as reasonably authoritative. It forms part of one of the manuscripts of Nennius (see below).

ANGLO-SAXON CHRONICLE. A summary history, year by year, first written down by the English in the ninth century during the reign of King Alfred. It made use of older material. For the period dealt with in this book it is therefore not a contemporary record, but contains the traditions of the Anglo-Saxons for the events described.

ANGLO-SAXON POETRY. There is a considerable volume of Anglo-Saxon poetry which throws light on the beliefs and attitudes of the first English. One poem—'The Ruin'—describes the emotions felt by the poet on seeing a deserted Roman building. This is the poem referred to in Chapter I.

ASHE, GEOFFREY: *FROM CAESAR TO ARTHUR.* This book deals very fully with all the evidence, literary as well as archaeological, of the period, and traces the story of Arthur. It is comprehensive and authoritative.

BEDE. The English historian who was writing in the eighth century. His *Ecclesiastical History of the English People* is a most careful and scholarly work. He made abundant use of older material and may be taken as a reliable authority.

CARMARTHEN, THE BLACK BOOK OF. This is so called because it was formerly kept at the Augustinian Priory at Carmarthen. Dating from the Norman period, it is the oldest Welsh manuscript in existence and contains a collection of early Welsh poems.

CASSIUS DIO. A Greek writer of the third century AD. He was a reliable historian, and gives an account of the invasion of Britain by the armies of the Emperor Claudius under Aulus Plautius in AD 43. He mentions Caractacus by name.

CHAMBERS, R. W. : *ENGLAND BEFORE THE NORMAN CONQUEST*. This gives extracts from the main source material.

CHRÉTIEN DE TROYES. A French poet of the twelfth century. He wrote five long poems dealing with Arthur and his knights. These are the earliest surviving Arthurian romances.

CLAUDIAN. A Latin poet born about the year 370 and dying around 404. He was a native of Alexandria, but settled in Italy. A protégé and supporter of Stilicho, he wrote many poems in celebration of the latter's exploits. These may well exaggerate Stilicho's achievements, but Claudian is a contemporary of the events he describes and therefore a most useful witness.

COLLINGWOOD, R. G. and MYERS, J. N. L. : *ROMAN BRITAIN AND THE ENGLISH SETTLEMENTS*. The first volume in the Oxford History of England. It gives a detailed and authoritative account of the period.

CRAWFORD, O. G. S. : *ANTIQUITY* No. IX, 1935. He identifies the site of the Battle of Camlann as Camboglanna, on the Wall.

EKWELL, E. : *THE CONCISE OXFORD DICTIONARY OF ENGLISH PLACE-NAMES*. An invaluable source of information on the origins and early spellings of the names of towns, villages and rivers in England.

EUMENIUS. A third-century writer from Gaul, author of a panegyric on Constantius Chlorus.

EUTROPIUS : *EPITOME OF ROMAN HISTORY*. Written in the fourth century. Tells of Saxon raids in the late third century, and gives an account of Carausius.

GEOFFREY OF MONMOUTH : *HISTORY OF THE BRITISH KINGS*. Geoffrey was a twelfth-century Welsh priest. He is more a romancer and writer of fables than a true historian, and his statements must be used with the greatest caution.

GERMANUS, S. F. : *THE LIFE OF GERMANUS* is a good and reliable document. Germanus was Bishop of Auxerre from 418 to 448. He visited Britain twice, and the *Life* not only gives an account of the Alleluia victory, but also throws an interesting light on conditions in Britain at that time.

GILDAS: *THE DESTRUCTION AND CONQUEST OF BRITAIN*. Gildas was a British monk, and this book was written during the fifth century. So he is a contemporary witness for the times of Arthur and his work, though hysterical in tone and obscure in language, must be given great weight.

THE LIFE OF ST GILDAS was written in Llancarfan in Ireland. The existing manuscript dates from the fourteenth century, but the document contains much older material.

GIRALDUS CAMBRENSIS. A Welsh ecclesiastical writer of considerable learning. He was born about 1146 and died about 1223. He wrote about the Wales of his own day, but included items of earlier periods.

GOODCHILD, R.: *ANTIQUITY* No. XXXIV, 1960. He gives a full account of the excavation of a palace in Cyrenaica which is approximately of the same date as Arthur, and which helps us to understand the kind of establishment which Arthur would have maintained.

HISTORIAE AUGUSTAE. A fourth-century collection of lives of the Emperors. It refers to the building of the Wall by Hadrian, and also gives a fairly full account of the campaign of Septimius Severus.

MALORY, SIR THOMAS: *MORTE D'ARTHUR*. This famous fifteenth-century collection of Arthurian legends was first printed by Caxton, who in his preface claims that Malory made use of many sources—English, French and others—to gather his information.

DE MIRABILIBUS BRITANNIAE. A treatise on the marvels of Britain, forming part of Nennius's work (see below). It is a collection of magical tales from many parts of Britain.

NENNIUS. He is said to be the author of the *HISTORY OF THE BRITONS* which first mentions Arthur by name. It was probably drawn up about 800 AD but is certainly based on older material. Some scholars have argued that he made use of a Romano-British work written in the late fifth century.

NOTITIA DIGNITATUM. The Roman government's list of civil and military officers throughout the Empire. There exist four copies, made in the fifteenth and sixteenth century, of an eleventh-century copy (now lost) of the Roman original. It is an accurate source of official information.

PROCOPIUS. A Byzantine writer of the sixth century. His account of Britain is full of strange tales and fables. However, we know that there were Angles serving in Constantinople, so some of his statements may be authentic.

'PROSPER TIRO'. The name given (erroneously) to a fifth-century chronicler in Southern Gaul. He describes the devastation of Britain by the Saxons in 410, and also describes Britain as having been subjugated by the Saxons in 442, which appears to be an exaggeration.

PTOLEMAEUS (Ptolemy the geographer). He lived in the second century and is the first writer to mention the Saxons.

TACITUS. A brilliant and reliable Roman writer of the first century AD. He had a special interest in Britain, being the son-in-law of Agricola, governor of Britain, whose biography he wrote. He also wrote *The Annals*, a history of Rome. He gives a full account both of Caractacus and of the revolt of Boudica. His other book *Germany*, contains an account of the manners and customs of the German tribes, amongst which he lists the Angli, some 350 years before they came to Britain. From him therefore we have something of the character, customs and religion of the first English.

TOYNBEE, J. M. C., Professor : *JOURNAL* of the British Archaeological Association, Vol. XVI, 1953. She gives a complete summary of the literary and archaeological evidence for Christianity in Roman Britain. In the *JOURNAL OF ROMAN STUDIES*, Vol. LIV, 1964, she identifies the portrait on a Roman fourth-century mosaic, found at Hinton St Mary, as probably that of Christ.

TRIADS. The *WELSH TRIADS (TRIOEDD YNYS PRY-DEIN)* are medieval poems recording names, facts and places in groups of three. They have been published by the University of Wales Press with introduction, translation and commentary by Rachel Bromwich.

WILLIAM OF MALMESBURY : *A CHRONICLE OF THE KINGS OF ENGLAND*. William was an English monk, and wrote his history in the early twelfth century. He was a diligent and careful scholar.

WHITE, D. A. : *LITUS SAXONICUM* (State Historical Society of Wisconsin). This is a very full study of the Saxon shore. The author concludes that the name was probably given because

Saxons were early settled there, rather than because this shore was being attacked by them.

ZOSIMUS. A fifth-century Byzantine writer. He records that Britain was compelled by the Saxons to leave the Empire, but adds that the Britons took up arms and freed their lands from the attacks of the barbarians. He also records the note of Honorius.

4: CHRONOLOGICAL SCHEME

AD
383 Maximus leads legions out of Britain
388 Maximus dies

---

410 Rome taken by Goths
420 (about) Hengist born
425-6 Vortigern's reign opens
427 (about) Ambrosius born
428 Existing version of *Notitia Dignitatum* compiled
429 St Germanus visits Britain. Alleluia victory
Saxons take Isle of Wight
435 Aetius defeats Burgundians
447 Saxons come to Britain as Treaty Troops
455 Hengist and Horsa fight Vortigern at battle of Aylesford
457 Saxons defeat Britons at Crayford
472 (about) Arthur born
473 Saxons break out from Kent
477 Aelle comes to Britain
488 Hengist dies
490 Saxons capture Pevensey
495 (or before) Ambrosius dies
Cerdic comes to Britain
Arthur in his early twenties

---

500 (about) Palace of Duke of Cyrenaica built
508 Battle of Charford; Saxons slay a British king
512 Uther Pendragon dies
Arthur appointed to leadership of Britain
Octha, Hengist's son, dies
514 Battle of Cerdic's-ore, in which Britons defeated

517 Battle of Badon (as proposed in this book)

537 Battle of Camlann
     Arthur dies

547 Maglocunnus dies. Gildas's book written before this date
     New Anglo-Saxon landings in the North

570 Gildas dies

577 Saxons take Gloucester, Cirencester and Bath

INDEX

Aaron, British martyr, 34

Adrianople, Battle of, 45, 61

Aelle, lands in Sussex, 89; captures Pevensey, 90; King of South Saxons, 190

Aesc, son of Hengist, 81; succeeds to Kingdom of Kent, 90; mentioned by Nennius, 95; as king (Octha), 147; death, 174

Aetius, consul in Rome, 70; Britons appeal to, 70; defeats Burgundians, 144

Agravaine, 135

Agrippa, 135

Alaric, 49, 57

Albans, St, *see* Verulamium

Albinus, *see* Clodius Albinus

Alemanni, in Britain, 39, 56, 185

Alexandria, 48

Alfred, King, 137, 191

Allectus, Emperor in Britain, 24, 26

Alleluia victory, 65; effect, 68

Ambrosius, origins, 69; interview with Vortigern, 76-8; emerges as leader, 79; career, 83-93; death, 91, 92, 173; progeny, 115; William of Malmesbury on, 171, 172

Anderida, *see* Pevensey

Aneurin, 149

Angles, invaders of Britain, 19; recorded by Tacitus, 22; called by Saxons to Britain as Treaty Troops, 74, 182; led by Hengist, 86

Anglo-Saxon Chronicle, 73, 203; on coming of the Saxons, 73, 74; on revolt of Treaty Troops, 75; on Battle of Aylesford, 78, 79; on defeat of Britons AD 473, 81; on events AD 473-490, 89; on death of Hengist, 90, 92, 174; on Aelle's victory, 90; on Battle of Charford, 91; on Cerdic, 91, 136-9, 186; on capture of towns in west, 108; on events after Badon, 120-2; on Wlencing's arrival in Britain, 131; on Leodwald, 134; peace AD 530-552, 178

Annales Cambriae, 116-17, 203; on Arthur's death, 18, 120, 172; on Gildas's death, 110, 120; on Battle of Badon, 117, 119; on Battle of Camlann, 176-8

Annals of Tigernach, 116

Antiquity, 165, 177

Aquileia, Battle of, 47, 48, 182

Arles, Council of, 34, 141

Armorica, Maximus's troops settle in, 47, 182; men from, 126

Army, Roman, enlistment, 37-9, 41; *see also* cavalry

Arthur, defender of Britain, 13, 18; myth of, 16-18; death, 18, 120, 172, 175-9; champions Christianity, 35, 65, 92-3, 117, 165, 167-9, 186; leads mounted men, 40, 93; considered as Maximus, 45-52; compared with Ambrosius, 92-4; battles, 95-122, 102 (map); hostility to, from Gildas, 112-16, 149-50; wife, 132-4; birth, 115, 170-1, 174, 197; as Duke of